Healthy Weight
for Teens

Healthy Weight
for Teens

CARLA MOONEY

LUCENT BOOKS
A part of Gale, Cengage Learning

GALE
CENGAGE Learning

Detroit • New York • San Francisco • New Haven, Conn • Waterville, Maine • London

LIBRARY OF CONGRESS CATALOGING-IN-PUBLICATION DATA

Mooney, Carla, 1970-
 Healthy weight for teens / by Carla Mooney.
   pages cm. -- (Nutrition and health)
 Summary: "Each title in the series delves into some of the hottest nutrition and health topics being discussed today. The series also provides readers with tools for evaluating conflicting and ever-changing ideas about nutrition and health"-- Provided by publisher.
 Includes bibliographical references and index.
 ISBN 978-1-4205-1021-8 (hardback)
 1. Teenagers--Nutrition--Juvenile literature. 2. Teenagers--Health and hygiene--Juvenile literature. 3. Youth--Nutrition--Juvenile literature. I. Title.
 RJ235.M66 2013
 613'.0433--dc23

                                                    2013001843

Lucent Books
27500 Drake Rd.
Farmington Hills, MI 48331

ISBN-13: 978-1-4205-1021-8
ISBN-10: 1-4205-1021-5

Printed in the United States of America
1 2 3 4 5 6 7 17 16 15 14 13

TABLE OF CONTENTS

Many people today are often amazed by the amount of nutrition and health information, often contradictory, that can be found in the media. Television, newspapers, and magazines bombard readers with the latest news and recommendations. Television news programs report on recent scientific studies. The healthy living sections of newspapers and magazines offer information and advice. In addition, electronic media such as websites, blogs, and forums post daily nutrition and health news and recommendations.

This constant stream of information can be confusing. The science behind nutrition and health is constantly evolving. Current research often leads to new ideas and insights. Many times, the latest nutrition studies and health recommendations contradict previous studies or traditional health advice. When the media reports these changes without giving context or explanations, consumers become confused. In a survey by the National Health Council, for example, 68 percent of participants agreed that "when reporting medical and health news, the media often contradict themselves, so I don't know what to believe." In addition, the Food Marketing Institute reported that eight out of ten consumers thought it was likely that nutrition and health experts would have a completely different idea about what foods are healthy within five years. With so much contradictory information, people have difficulty deciding how to apply nutrition and health recommendations to their lives. Students find it difficult to find relevant, yet clear and credible information for reports.

Changing recommendations for antioxidant supplements are an example of how confusion can arise. In the 1990s antioxidants such as vitamins C and E and beta-carotene came to the public's attention. Scientists found that people who ate more antioxidant-rich foods had a lower risk of heart disease, cancer, vision loss, and other chronic conditions than those who ate lower amounts. Without waiting for more scientific study, the media and supplement companies quickly spread the word that antioxidants could help fight and prevent disease. They recommended that people take antioxidant supplements and eat fortified foods. When further scientific studies were completed, however, most did not support the initial recommendations. While naturally occurring antioxidants in fruits and vegetables may help prevent a variety of chronic diseases, little scientific evidence proved antioxidant supplements had the same effect. In fact, a study published in the November 2008 *Journal of the American Medical Association* found that supplemental vitamins A and C gave no more heart protection than a placebo. The study's results contradicted the widely publicized recommendation, leading to consumer confusion. This example highlights the importance of context for evaluating nutrition and health news. Understanding a topic's scientific background, interpreting a study's findings, and evaluating news sources are critical skills that help reduce confusion.

Lucent's Nutrition and Health series is designed to help young people sift through the mountain of confusing facts, opinions, and recommendations. Each book contains the most recent up-to-date information, synthesized and written so that students can understand and think critically about nutrition and health issues. Each volume of the series provides a balanced overview of today's hot-button nutrition and health issues while presenting the latest scientific findings and a discussion of issues surrounding the topic. The series provides young people with tools for evaluating conflicting and ever-changing ideas about nutrition and health. Clear narrative peppered with personal anecdotes, fully documented primary and secondary source quotes, informative sidebars, fact boxes, and statistics are all used to help readers understand these topics and how they affect their bodies and their lives. Each volume includes information about changes in trends over time, political controversies, and international perspectives. Full-color photographs and charts enhance all volumes in the series. The Nutrition and Health series is a valuable resource for young people to understand current topics and make informed choices for themselves.

Teens and Weight Loss

Today's teens face enormous pressure to be thin. Everywhere teens look, billboards, commercials, magazines, movies, and television shows promote models and actors that are skinnier than ever. In some cases media images are even altered digitally to create an unrealistic image that is impossible for a real teen to attain. At the same time, the news media and spokespeople from health organizations warn about the epidemic of obesity that is overtaking Americans. Dire predictions about the effect of extra weight on the future health of today's teens are regular features in newspapers, magazines, and the television news. Each story adds further pressure on teens to think about weight loss, regardless of their actual size.

While they are trying to fit into size 0 jeans, teens are being tempted to eat more and exercise less. Portion sizes have increased tremendously over the past decades. Practically everything from sodas to candy bars can be supersized. No longer satisfied with a simple cup of coffee, teens drop by trendy coffeehouses for the latest coffee creation, regardless of the number of calories and grams of fat in each sip. In addition, technology has made it easy for teens to go through the day without breaking a sweat. Today's favorite teen pastimes—texting, social networking, playing video games, and downloading the latest digital content—are making teens more sedentary than ever.

With so many mixed messages, it is not surprising that many teens are confused about weight and dieting. Messages urging them to be thin are delivered next to advertisements for the latest high-calorie, low-nutrient food. To make it even more confusing, health experts warn teens about the risks of obesity, but they also recommend that children and teens should not diet. Restricting food and calories during adolescence can stunt growth, delay maturation, and have long-lasting negative health consequences. In addition, psychologists warn that promoting diets to young people, especially girls, may increase the number of adolescents who develop unhealthy eating habits and eating disorders.

While society gives teens the message to stay thin and healthy, it also tempts them to eat more and exercise less.

With all of this conflicting information, teens are sure to be confused and unsure about how to be healthy and satisfied with their weight and body image. Haley Lacey is a registered dietitian who treats children and teens. She says teens need to focus less on weight and more on health. "It is important for teens to remember that finding a healthy weight should be about health," she says. "For teens to lose weight the right way, it is imperative to focus on eating for fuel, to give the body energy, and to eat to promote health."[1]

CHAPTER 1

Healthy Weight and Body Image

When sixteen-year-old Kenderick S. was younger, he was not at a healthy weight. He got tired quickly, and kids at school teased him about his weight. "I didn't do the things I enjoyed, because I was self-conscious about my weight," he says. When his twenty-five-year-old brother had a heart attack, Kenderick realized that he needed to make some changes in his life to bring his weight to a more healthy level. He started by eating less junk food and adding more exercise to his daily routine. Before long Kenderick had lost 40 pounds (18kg) and reached a healthier weight. "It was very hard work, but the rewards have changed my life,"[2] he says.

Achieving a healthy weight is a goal that is becoming harder for Americans. According to the Centers for Disease Control and Prevention (CDC), about 36 percent of American adults over age twenty are obese, while an additional 33 percent are overweight. In addition, approximately 18 percent of adolescents aged twelve to nineteen are obese. The trend of obesity is increasing. A 2012 CDC report projects that about 42 percent of the U.S. population will become obese by 2030. At the same time, some Americans are struggling with the opposite problem; they are underweight and cannot gain weight despite their

efforts. According to data collected by the Natior
for Health Statistics, almost 2 percent of Americ
are underweight.

Experts are particularly concerned about risir
because extra weight has a significant effect on
couple of extra pounds of body fat is not a healt
body fat accumulates, however, it can reach a poir
has a negative effect on health. Being overweigh
increases a person's risk of developing type 2 diab
disease, stroke, several types of cancer, kidney fa
other chronic illnesses. Being obese can have e
serious health consequences. The risk of death fro
cancers increases as a person becomes more obese
ing to the CDC report's authors, people who are o

Child Obesity Statistics & Teenage Obesity Statistics by Age and Gender

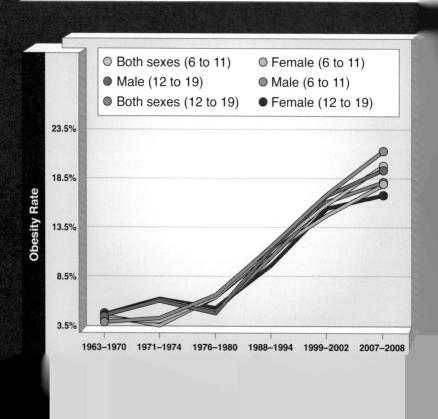

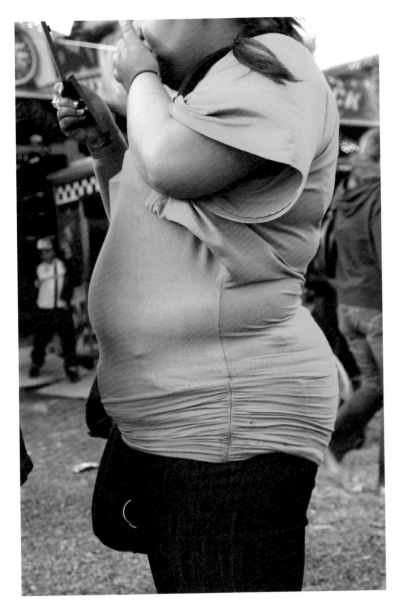

Being obese increases a person's risk of developing type 2 diabetes, heart disease, stroke, cancer, kidney failure, and other illnesses.

have a much shorter life expectancy and will incur greater lifetime medical costs.

Although it may be difficult to do, achieving and maintaining a healthy weight has many benefits. A person who maintains a healthy weight is more likely to prevent and control many diseases and conditions. Being at a healthy weight can also help people feel good about themselves and have more energy to participate in favorite activities.

What Is a Healthy Weight?

Not everyone has to be stick thin to be healthy. "People come in all shapes and sizes,"[3] says Marc Jacobson, a professor of pediatric medicine at Albert Einstein College of Medicine in New York City. Whether a person is big, tall, petite, or curvy, there is a wide range of healthy weights. Genetics, gender, nutrition, physical activity, and health conditions can all influence a person's height and weight.

Two people who are the same height and age can have different body types and weights. Some people are more muscular or have larger bones than others have. Youth who have gone through puberty may have a different body shape than peers who have not. Even heredity can affect a person's body shape and weight. People from different races, ethnic groups, and nationalities can have different body fat distribution (where the fat is located on the body). They can also have different body compositions or amounts of bone, muscle, and fat. An athlete may have a higher weight because he or she has a higher percentage of dense muscle tissue, while a less active person of the same height may have a higher body fat percentage. Although healthy weight comes in many shapes and sizes, some people are outside of these healthy ranges. A person is overweight or obese if he or she has extra or excessive body fat that may impair his or her health.

Because a healthy weight is not simply a number on a scale, many people talk to a doctor or a dietitian to help determine what weight is healthy for them. For children and teens that are still growing, doctors often use a healthy weight range based on height and age. Teens in particular are going through a period of rapid growth. Their bodies may gain weight rapidly but remain healthy if body fat, muscle, and bone remain in proportion.

To track weight over time, pediatricians can use pediatric growth charts developed by the CDC for children aged two through nineteen. These charts track height and weight over time and show how a child is growing compared with other kids of the same age and gender. There is no single ideal number; instead, doctors look to see whether a child is following the same growth pattern over time and whether height and weight are in proportion to each other.

Body Mass Index

Because people have different body compositions, doctors do not rely on a scale alone to determine whether a person falls within a healthy weight range. A tool called the body mass index (BMI) can also help. BMI is a formula that allows doctors to estimate how much body fat a person has on the basis of his or her weight and height. "BMI puts the height and weight into a ratio that helps us figure out if one is too heavy for their height or too skinny for their height,"[4] says Kristi King, a registered dietitian at Texas Children's Hospital.

Having a high BMI, however, does not always mean a person is unhealthy. "It is important to note that these are just guidelines as muscle weighs more than fat so if there is an athlete who has high muscle mass, they may plot out high on the growth curve,"[5] says King. BMI should be used as an indicator along with other information, such as diet, physical activity, family history, and other health screenings.

A doctor checks a patient's body mass index (BMI), a ratio of a person's weight to his or her height.

For adults aged twenty and over, the BMI number is read using standard categories. A BMI below 18.5 is considered underweight, 18.5 to 24.9 is normal, 25.0 to 29.9 is overweight, and 30.0 and above is obese. These categories are the same for adult males and females.

For children and teens, BMI is interpreted differently. Normal body fat amounts differ between girls and boys and change as children age. For these reasons, doctors often use a BMI growth chart that is age- and gender-specific. These charts translate a BMI number into a percentile, which indicates where a child's or teen's BMI number falls among children of the same sex and age. The BMI charts also show whether a child or teen falls into a healthy weight range or whether he or she is underweight, overweight, or obese. The large majority of children and teens fall into a healthy weight range, from the 5th to less than the 85th percentile, and represent a wide range of sizes and shapes. Those who fall into the extreme ends of the BMI chart—either underweight or overweight—may be at greater risk for health problems that impact their lives.

Weight Status Category	Percentile Range
Underweight	Less than the 5th percentile
Healthy weight	5th percentile to less than the 85th percentile
Overweight	85th to less than the 95th percentile
Obese	Equal to or greater than the 95th percentile

Because children and teens are growing and changing so quickly, a single height, weight, or BMI measurement is not as useful as several measurements tracked over time. One red flag that a child may not be at a healthy weight is when a child's height and weight do not increase at the same rate. For example, if a boy's height remains in the 30th percentile (that is, he is taller than thirty out of one hundred boys his age) and his weight increases to the 80th percentile (he weighs more than eighty out of one hundred boys his age), he may be at an unhealthy weight. Also, if a teen has a high BMI measurement for his or her age and sex, a doctor may perform further health assessments. The doctor may ask questions about the teen's diet, physical activity, and family history. Using all of this information, the doctor will determine whether the teen is in a healthy weight range or whether he or she should make lifestyle changes to become healthier.

Body Image

No matter what the number on a scale or BMI chart reads, many teens do not feel good about their bodies and themselves. They worry about how they look to others—are they too fat or too skinny? Are their thighs too large or their shoulders too small? These teens are struggling with their body image. According to Purdue University sociology researcher Sarah Mustillo, body image "is an individual's perceptions, thoughts and feelings about her body, and how they're shaped through interactions with others and within a larger societal context."[6]

Concern over appearance is not a new phenomenon. Throughout history, people have judged themselves against their society's standard of beauty. Every society throughout history has had its own set of ideals regarding physical characteristics and what is considered attractive. Beauty characteristics are not static; they change and adapt over time. For example, the ideal female shape in 1950s magazines was curvier than the models used today.

In addition, different cultures have different standards for body size and shape. Some cultures celebrate a fuller body shape than others. In fact, in some places in Africa, being fat is desirable because it is associated with abundance and fertility. "Culturally speaking, the ideal body shape is a lean one among Asian children. In African-American and Latino cultures, being lean is not always the ideal,"[7] says Gary Foster, a researcher at the Center for Obesity Research

and Education at Temple University who has studied body image in youth from different cultures. These variations can affect how a teen views his or her body image. Teens from more accepting cultures are more likely to have positive body images.

When a teen has a negative body image, it often affects how he or she views healthy weight. Teens with poor body image may think of themselves as fat and try to lose weight, even if they are at a normal weight. "Our societal ideal for the ideal body is unrealistic and often times, underweight. Teens are being led to believe that they must diet and be 'skinny' in order to be 'ok' and as a result, weight loss is no longer about being healthy and taking care of yourself, but instead transforms into a way to punish yourself or an act of desperation that is linked to self worth,"[8] says Rebecca Clegg, a licensed professional counselor who specializes in helping people overcome unhealthy eating patterns and body image issues.

Unrealistic Images in the Media Affect Body Image

The media is a powerful influence on a teen's body image. Teens are surrounded by images of celebrities and models in magazines, movies, and television. Many teenage girls compare themselves to the images that they perceive to be beautiful. According to a 2008 study conducted by the Girl Scout Research Institute, 73 percent of girls compare how they look to girls in the media sometimes, while 29 percent compared their looks to media images a lot or all the time. "Pictures of beautiful, thin, rich actresses and models certainly affect how teens feel about themselves. When teenagers see these women and girls, it can make them feel badly about themselves and may provide an unhealthy ideal weight,"[9] says dietitian Haley Lacey.

Many people are concerned that the media is presenting unrealistic body images to teens. According to the CDC, the average American woman is about five feet four inches tall and weighs more than 150 pounds (68kg). In comparison, the average model is much taller and thinner and has significantly less body fat. In recent years the disparity between real life and media images has gotten worse. According to statistics from the Rader Eating Disorder Programs, twenty years ago the average fashion model weighed 8 percent less than the average woman. Today the average model weighs 23 percent less. While about 50 percent of women in America wear a size 14 or larger, in the fashion industry a size 6 is considered a plus size for a model. In fact, many fashion runway models are so thin that they meet BMI criteria for being anorexic, or suffering from an eating disorder characterized by an obsessive desire to lose weight. In addition, models spend hours with hair and makeup professionals to look flawless. Digital manipulation of images can make models and celebrities look thinner, whiten their teeth, and erase wrinkles and blemishes.

Comparing themselves to these unrealistic images can negatively affect

HEALTH FACT

Most fashion models are thinner than 98 percent of American women.

how teens feel about their bodies. In some cases having a negative body image can lead to a teen developing an eating disorder. Eating disorders such as anorexia, bulimia, and binge eating disorder are complex and serious illnesses. People with eating disorders are generally obsessed with food, weight, and appearance. Eating disorders can lead to serious health problems and in some cases even death.

According to an online survey of one thousand girls between the ages of thirteen and seventeen conducted by

Moderate Versus Vigorous Activity

The U.S. Department of Health and Human Services recommends that teens be physically active for at least sixty minutes per day to get to and stay at a healthy weight. The department also recommends that most of that sixty minutes be made up of aerobic activity of both moderate and vigorous intensity, such as swimming or running that is designed to improve the body's use of oxygen.

Moderate-intensity aerobic activity causes breathing and heart rate to increase, but at a level at which a teen can still carry on a conversation. Examples of moderate-intensity activity include:

- Brisk walking at a fifteen-minute-mile pace
- Light yard work such as raking or bagging leaves or pushing a lawn mower
- Shoveling snow
- Active play with children
- Casual biking

Vigorous activity raises the heart rate substantially, causing a person to breathe too hard and fast to have a conversation. Examples of vigorous-intensity activities include:

- Jogging or running
- Swimming laps
- Rollerblading at a fast pace
- Cross-country skiing
- Jumping rope
- Competitive sports such as soccer, basketball, or football

the Girl Scouts of the USA in 2010, almost nine out of ten American teenage girls say they feel pressured by the fashion and media industries to be skinny and that the media create an unrealistic, unattainable image of beauty. "The fashion industry remains a powerful influence on girls and the way they view themselves and their bodies," says Kimberlee Salmond, a senior researcher at the Girl Scout Research Institute. "Teenage girls take cues about how they should look from models they see in fashion magazines and on TV and it is something that they struggle to reconcile with when they look at themselves in the mirror."[10]

Finding a Comfortable Body Weight

Health professionals recommend that teens focus on what makes them feel comfortable and happy in their own bodies instead of comparing themselves with others. A comfortable body weight is a weight that allows a teen to feel good about himself or herself. It is a weight that a teen does not have to starve or exercise obsessively to maintain. It is also a healthy weight, so that the teen has no medical problems caused by his or her weight.

Sometimes a person's comfortable weight may not be what others tell him or her it should be. Sari M. is a teen who has lost about 20 pounds (9kg) and is comfortable at her

Health experts think teens should focus on healthy eating and physical activities instead of setting a weight goal that may be unrealistic or even unobtainable.

Reading Nutrition Labels

In 1990 federal regulation required food companies to put nutrition information on their food packaging in a standardized way. Nutrition Facts labels tell people how big a serving size is and how many servings are in a package. They also provide information about the levels of calories, fat, carbohydrates, sodium, fiber, sugars, and protein in the food. Labels also give the levels of any vitamins or minerals in the food. A second column on the label calculates the percentage of the recommended daily value for a nutrient. For example, a 1.5-ounce (43g) box of raisins contains 33 grams of carbohydrates, or 11 percent of the recommended daily value. In addition, food labels list the ingredients in the food. The list is ordered from greatest to least.

Some food labels, however, are misleading. In addition to the required Nutrition Facts label, food manufacturers can print claims like "low fat," "reduced," or "light" on packaging. Sometimes these foods are not as healthy as the manufacturer claims. Some foods use several types of sugars and list them separately on the food label. Separated into smaller-sized groups, the sugars can be buried farther down on the ingredient list. Some gummy snacks claim on their packages that they are made with fruit. The claim is technically true, but some might have the equivalent of only two grapes in each package. The rest is sugar. Even the labels on milk can be deceiving. Two percent milk cartons claim the milk is low fat. However, most people do not know that milk is exempt from labeling laws that say a product has to have 3 grams of fat or less per serving to be called low fat. Two percent milk has 5 grams of fat per serving. Three of those grams are unhealthy saturated fats.

Food packaging labels provide facts on the food's key nutrient content, as well as calorie content and serving size.

Nutrition Facts

Serving Size 2 Cakes/1 Pkg (60g)
Servings Per Container 6

Amount Per Serving

Calories 220	Calories from Fat 70	
		% Daily Value*
Total Fat 7g		**11%**
Saturated Fat 2.5g		**13%**
Trans Fat 0g		
Cholesterol 10mg		**3%**
Sodium 270mg		**11%**
Total Carbohydrate 36g		**12%**
Dietary Fiber 2g		**7%**
Sugars 27g		
Protein 2g		

current weight of 144 pounds (65kg). She says, "I realized that as long as I look good in my clothes and feel happy and good in general, the 'ideal' weight doesn't matter much." She advises teens to "figure out what your desired weight range is and make sure it's healthy."[11]

Some health experts advise against teens setting a weight goal. Instead, they feel that teens should focus on healthy eating and activity behaviors, which will naturally lead to a healthy weight. "Rather than pick a weight number ahead of time, teens should see what happens when they eat and exercise reasonably,"[12] says Craig Johnson, director of the Eating Disorders Program at Laureate Psychiatric Clinic and Hospital in Tulsa, Oklahoma. Other experts recommend that teens set a weight range or clothing size that is realistic for their body type and shape, instead of a specific number on a scale.

When Is Weight Loss Appropriate for Teens?

For some teens, simply maintaining their current weight as they grow taller is a sensible way to achieve a healthy weight over time. Growing teens who are considered overweight (with BMI scores in the 85th to 95th percentile) without any medical problems caused by their weight are generally advised to maintain weight rather than start a weight loss program. These teens will grow into a healthy weight range as they adopt a lifestyle that includes physical activity and healthy eating. "Many teenage girls are still growing taller, so for them, maintaining weight or slowing weight gain is an acceptable goal,"[13] says Phil Wu, a pediatrician who focuses on preventing and treating childhood obesity.

For some teens, a plan for safe, gradual weight loss may be appropriate to achieve a healthy weight. Teens who may be good candidates for a gradual weight loss plan include those with BMI scores in the 95th percentile or higher or teens with BMI scores in the 85th to 95th percentile who have medical problems related to their weight. Experts agree that any weight loss plan for teens should be gradual, with slow and steady loss of no more than 1 to 2 pounds (454g to 907g) per week. Lacey advises:

> The spectrum of safe weight loss for teens depends on how much extra weight is present, and where the teen is in his or her growth cycle. If a teen hasn't yet

reached full height, extreme calorie restriction may stunt height. In general if a teen has reached full adult height, a pound a week is a safe rate of weight loss. Teens should never restrict calories to less than 1,200 per day, or cut out entire food groups from the diet.[14]

There is no number on a scale that is right for everyone. When trying to establish a healthy weight, teens should talk to a doctor or dietitian to set realistic and healthy goals.

CHAPTER 2

Healthy Habits for a Healthy Weight

People looking to lose weight often adopt the latest fad diet or exercise craze. Diets that have participants eating cabbage soup or eliminating all carbohydrates may seem like a quick way to drop weight. Yet fad diets often backfire. Experts advise that there is no magic bullet for achieving and maintaining a healthy weight. Over time, the most successful way to achieve a long-term healthy weight is to adopt healthy eating habits and increase physical activity. "Exercise, a healthy diet, and changing behaviors is what is going to make a difference and help kids lose weight and keep it off,"[15] says Kerri Boutelle, an adolescence and obesity expert at the University of Minnesota.

Keeping a Body in Balance

Food provides the energy that charges a teen's body for the day. During the day, the body uses energy to think and move. People eat regularly to keep their energy levels up. The process of getting energy from food is called metabolism. This is a series of chemical reactions in the body's cells that convert the fuel from food into the energy needed for everyday activity. People at a healthy weight manage to balance the energy they take in (food) with the energy they use (activity).

A calorie is a unit of heat energy in food. One calorie provides the energy needed to warm the temperature of 1 gram of water 1 degree Celsius. Without the energy in calories, a person could not walk, talk, move, or think. Therefore, calories are not bad; they are necessary to live a healthy lifestyle. Dianne Neumark-Sztainer, a researcher and professor at the School of Public Health at the University of Minnesota who studies adolescent eating behaviors, explains:

> Our bodies need energy even just for things like breathing. Calories are simply a measure of the energy in the food we eat. You're still growing, so your body needs more energy, but once you stop growing, you'll need less. When you are more active, such as during the soccer season, you need more energy, but during the winter when you're not doing a sport, you need less. It's a matter of balance.[16]

To maintain weight, calorie intake should equal calories used for physical activity and everyday body processes. There is no right number of calories for everyone. The number of calories a person needs depends on his or her gender, age, and activity levels. If a teen does not consume enough calories, he or she will lose weight and have low energy and may be unable to participate in the activities he or she enjoys. If a teen eats too many calories, he or she will gain weight and may experience other health problems.

In addition, all calories are not created equal. Two foods may have the same number of calories, but one may have more nutrients that the body needs to function properly. Nutrients are the components of food that are needed by the body for energy and tissue building. For example, a candy bar can pack 250 calories but has little to offer in terms of vitamins, protein, or other nutrients. Instead, its calories come from sugars that have little nutritional value. On the other hand, an apple with two tablespoons of peanut butter has about the same number of calories as the candy bar, but it also provides fiber, vitamins, and protein, all of which are essential to healthy body function.

Calories are a measure of the energy in foods. One calorie equals the energy needed to raise the temperature of one gram of water by one degree Celsius.

What Is Healthy Eating?

Healthy eating is one of the keys to living at a healthy weight. Today's teens are surrounded by fast and easy food choices. French fries, chips, and candy bars are all easy options to stave off hunger during a packed schedule. Yet research has shown that for teens to be at a healthy weight and in good overall health, they need to eat balanced meals and healthy snacks. Healthy eating is eating the right kinds of foods that provide essential nutrients and minimal amounts of added sugar and fat. Healthy eating is important because it allows the body to function optimally now and in the future. People who follow healthy eating plans can reduce their chances for many chronic diseases such as type 2 diabetes and cardiovascular disease. For children and teens, healthy eating provides the energy and nutrients that make them feel good and perform well, improve their overall health, and provide the essential building blocks their bodies need to grow and develop. Healthy eating and regular physical activity also help teens achieve healthy weight and body composition.

Because healthy eating is so important for children and teens, many experts advise against children and teens actively dieting and restricting food and nutrient intake. During the teen years, adolescents grow the final 15 to 20 percent of their adult height while gaining about 50 percent of their adult body weight and up to 40 percent of their adult skeletal mass. During these critical growth years, inadequate nutrition can delay maturation, slow or stop growth, and interfere with bone development.

Five Food Groups

To eat healthfully, nutrition experts recommend that teens eat a variety of foods from five main food groups. The five food groups are the building blocks for a healthy eating plan.

Every five years, the U.S. Department of Agriculture and the U.S. Department of Health and Human Services publish the Dietary Guidelines for Americans, which provide information about the five food groups and healthy eating. The guidelines are based on an expert review of research related to eating, physical activity, and health.

Under the Dietary Guidelines, the five food groups are vegetables, fruits, grains, dairy, and proteins. Vegetables

HEALTH FACT

It would take about an hour of playing basketball to burn off the 550 calories in a McDonald's Big Mac sandwich.

A Healthy Plate of Food

MyPlate offers dietary guidelines for serving sizes of grains, fruits, vegetables, dairy products, and proteins.

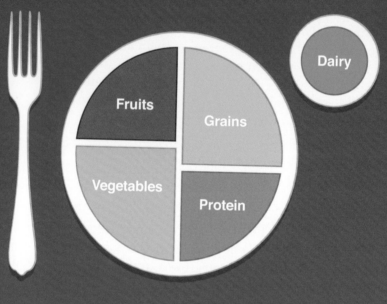

and fruits are low in calories but offer a wide variety of vitamins and minerals, which are necessary for healthy hair, eyes, nails, and immune system function. Most fruits and vegetables are high in fiber, which is good for digestion and helps the body feel fuller longer.

Grains provide carbohydrates, which are the body's main energy source. There are two main types of grains: whole and refined. Whole grains such as whole-wheat bread, brown rice, and whole-grain cereals are a good source of fiber. According to the Dietary Guidelines, at least half of the grains consumed should be whole grains. Refined grains include white bread, white rice, and pasta.

The protein group includes meat, beans, poultry, fish, eggs, nuts, and seeds. The body uses protein to build and repair cells, enzymes, and hormones. Proteins help the body form new blood cells, tissues, and muscle. For healthy eating, the Dietary Guidelines recommend that people eat the leanest cuts of meat and poultry, along with protein sources that provide healthy oils, such as fish, nuts, and seeds.

The dairy group includes milk and foods made from milk, such as yogurt and cheese. Dairy foods are an important source of calcium and vitamin D, which the body uses to build strong bones and teeth. Healthy dairy choices are fat-free or low-fat products.

Although not an official food group, some oils are part of a healthy diet when eaten in moderation. Oils are fats that are liquid at room temperature. They are primarily found in some vegetables, nuts, seeds, and fish. Oils are the body's main source of vitamin E, an antioxidant that helps brain development and fights inflammation in the body. Healthy oils contain polyunsaturated fatty acids and monounsaturated fatty acids that lower the levels of blood cholesterol. Examples of healthy oils include canola, corn, and olive oil and the oils found in tuna, salmon, nuts, and seeds.

Some foods do not fall into any of the five food groups. Items such as unhealthy oils, sodas, butter and margarine, and candy are high in solid fat, added sugar, and calories and do not provide nutrients that teens need. Experts recommend limiting consumption of these items.

MyPlate for Healthy Eating

In 2011 the U.S. government introduced MyPlate, a visual tool for healthy eating. It is based on the Dietary Guidelines created by the Department of Agriculture and the Department of Health and Human Services. The MyPlate icon is a snapshot of how the five food groups should be proportioned for healthy eating. The plate is split into four sections, for fruits, vegetables, grains, and protein. Fruits and vegetables fill half the plate, grains fill a little more than one-fourth, and protein such as lean meats and beans fills the remaining roughly one-fourth of the plate space. In addition, a small circle to the right represents dairy products such as milk or yogurt. "This is a quick, simple reminder for all of us to be more mindful of the foods that we're eating," said First Lady Michelle Obama at a news conference to unveil the new MyPlate guide. "We're all bombarded with so many dietary messages that it's hard to find time to sort through all this information, but we do have time to take a look at our kids' plates."[17]

The MyPlate icon reminds teens and adults what healthy eating looks like. A plate loaded with fruits and vegetables, like the MyPlate icon, is a healthy start. It is a "simple, visual, research-based icon that is a clear, unmistakable message about portion size,"[18] says agriculture secretary Tom Vilsack. Although it is a helpful reminder, the simple picture does not tell teens everything they need to know about what types of foods to eat for a healthy weight. For this reason, the Department of Agriculture created a website, www.choosemyplate .gov, which has more information about healthy eating for a healthy weight.

Calorie Counting

For some people, counting calories can be an effective tool for weight management. One pound (454g) of body fat has about thirty-five hundred calories of potential energy. If the number of calories consumed equals the amount of energy expended, weight will remain constant. If a person consumes 250 fewer calories per day and increases daily calorie burn by 250 calories through exercise, he or she can expect to lose about a pound of body weight in a week (500 fewer calories per day times seven days equals 3,500 calories, or a pound). On the other hand, if the same person consumes more calories than he or she burns, the result will be weight gain. Knowing the calorie count of different foods can help a person plan for healthy eating.

Some health professionals caution that there are pitfalls to overreliance on calorie counting, especially for teens. If only calories are considered, a person may not make overall healthy decisions. "I remember thinking, as a teen, 'Oh, I'll have a chocolate bar instead of a sandwich since it has fewer calories.' The problem was that in an hour I would

MyPlate Recommended Serving Sizes

The recommended serving sizes for MyPlate are based on the Dietary Guidelines for Americans. MyPlate serving sizes are given for each food group.

Grains: Recommended serving size = 1 ounce. Examples include a slice of bread, one cup of ready-to-eat cereal, one-half cup cooked rice, pasta, or cooked cereal.

Fruits: Recommended serving size = 1 cup. Examples include 1 cup sliced fruit, one-half cup dried fruit, 1 piece of whole fruit about the size of a tennis ball.

Vegetables: Recommended serving size = 1 cup. Examples include 1 cup raw or cooked vegetables, 1 cup vegetable juice, or 2 cups of leafy greens.

Dairy: Recommended serving size = 1 cup. Examples include 1 cup milk, 1 cup yogurt, or 1.5 ounces of natural cheese.

Proteins: Recommended serving size = 1 ounce. Examples include 1 ounce of meat, poultry, or fish; one-quarter cup cooked beans; one egg, 1 tablespoon peanut butter, or one-half ounce nuts or seeds.

MyPlate offers dietary guidelines for serving sizes of grains, fruits, vegetables, dairy products, and proteins.

be hungry again. Plus, the sandwich could have supplied a lot more nutrients per calorie than a chocolate bar,"[19] says Neumark-Sztainer. For this reason, many experts recommend that teens focus more on eating proper portions than on counting calories.

Inside the tablet screen:

Calorie Counter
fatsecret

- Q Search
- Barcode Scan
- Foods
- Restaurants & Chains
- Popular Brands
- Supermarket Brands
- Food Diary
- Exercise Diary
- Diet Calendar
- Weight Tracker
- Sync
- Settings

2:18 PM

Chocolate Chip Cookie

Food Info

Chocolate Chip Cookie

Serving Size **1 medium (approx 2" dia)**

Nutrition Info

Calories: 49
Total Fat: 2.47g
Total Carb: 6.41g
Protein: 0.55g

(Calories from Fat: 22)
(Saturated Fat: 0.77g)
(Sugar: 3.43g Fiber: 0.3g)

3% of RDI*
(49 calories)
*Based on an RDI of 1,900 calories

Add to My Food Diary

Date	Thursday, January 5
Meal	Breakfast
Description	Chocolate Chip Cookie

A girl uses an iPad calorie counter app to measure her daily caloric intake. For some people, calorie counting can be an effective tool for managing weight.

Proper Portions

The second part of healthy eating is eating the right amount, or the proper portion, of healthy foods. A portion is the amount of food that a person eats at one time. Some health experts suggest that practicing portion control is an effective way for teens to eat healthfully. "Although the balance between energy intake and expenditure is what ultimately determines whether one loses, maintains, or gains weight, too much focus on counting calories can backfire and be harmful. . . . Keeping an eye on portion size—without getting obsessed about it—is a good alternative to counting calories,"[20] says Neumark-Sztainer.

Portion size is not the same for everyone. The amount of food needed from each food group depends on a

Portion Overload

Portion sizes have increased dramatically over the past twenty years. Here is a look at some of the differences, according to the National Institutes of Health.

Then: A coffee with whole milk and sugar was 8 ounces and 45 calories.
Now: A typical 16-ounce cup of mocha coffee has 350 calories.

Then: A blueberry muffin measured 1.5 ounces and had 210 calories.
Now: Today's mega-sized blueberry muffins are a whopping 5 ounces and 500 calories.

Then: Two slices of pepperoni pizza had 500 calories.
Now: Two large pepperoni pizza slices have 850 calories.

Then: A chicken Caesar salad was 1.5 cups and had 390 calories.
Now: A typical portion of three cups of chicken Caesar salad has 790 calories.

Then: A box of popcorn held about 5 cups of popcorn and had 270 calories.
Now: A tub of air-popped popcorn at the movies holds about 20 cups of popcorn and has 630 calories.

Serving Size	Visual Guideline
A medium apple or peach is about the size of a tennis ball.	
1 ounce of cheese is about the size of 4 stacked dice.	
1/2 cup of ice cream is about the size of a tennis ball.	
1 cup of mashed potatoes or broccoli is about the size of your fist.	
1 teaspoon of butter or peanut butter is about the size of the tip of your thumb.	
1 ounce of nuts or small candies equals one handful.	= 1 oz.

Taken from: National Dairy Council.

person's age, gender, and level of physical activity. For example, teens who participate in sports may have higher energy needs and require larger portion sizes than less active teens. Males generally need larger portions than females to maintain a healthy weight. Sometimes, a person's healthy portions can change depending on his or her circumstances. A teen may need to eat more in the middle of basketball season to fuel his or her body through grueling three-hour daily practices than he or she needs to eat during the off-season.

In recent decades American portions have grown supersized. According to the New York City Department of Health and Mental Hygiene, the size of a beverage at a fast food chain has quadrupled since 1955, from 7 ounces to 32 ounces (198g to 907g). Over the same period, french fry portions have more than doubled, from 2.4 ounces to 5.4 ounces (68g to 153g). As a result of these ballooning portion sizes, some single restaurant meals today provide more calories than an adult requires for an entire day.

Even small increases in portion size can have an effect on weight and health. A daily increase of one hundred calories can lead to a weight gain of more than 10 pounds (4.5kg) in a year. "Super-sized portions at restaurants have distorted what Americans consider a normal portion size, and that affects how much we eat at home as well," says Elizabeth G. Nabel, director of the National Institutes of Health's National Heart, Lung, and Blood Institute. "One way to keep calories in check is to keep food portions no larger than the size of your fist."[21] Research has shown that the larger the portion, the more people eat. Eating too much of anything, even healthy food, can lead to weight gain.

To understand portion control, it is important to know the distinction between portion size and serving size. A serving is a specific amount of food or drink that is defined by common measurements such as cups, ounces, or tablespoons. Portion size is the actual amount of food on the plate. A portion can be bigger or smaller than

HEALTH FACT

The number one source of calories in the American diet is desserts.

the recommended serving size. The Department of Agriculture's MyPlate has recommended serving sizes for the five food groups and oils. The serving sizes on MyPlate are based on the Dietary Guidelines for Americans and consider the nutrients and calories in specific foods. Following the MyPlate serving guidelines is a good way for teens to establish a healthy eating plan.

One recommendation for determining a healthy portion of food is to eat no more of a food than the size of one's fist.

Because Americans are used to seeing enormous portions on plates, they often have a difficult time estimating how much food equals one recommended serving. If a teen overestimates the serving size, he or she will consume more calories than planned, which can lead to weight gain. For example, a typical muffin today is 4.5 ounces (128g). Because a MyPlate serving of grains is only 1.5 ounces (43g), the single muffin will actually count as three servings.

Measuring is the most accurate way to understand how much food is in a proper serving. However, measuring cups and spoons are not always available, particularly if a teen is not at home. In these situations teens can use familiar objects such as a tennis ball or CD that are a similar size to the recommended serving size in order to estimate a proper portion. For example, a 1-ounce (28g) serving of bread is about the size of a CD cover. A one-quarter cup serving of raisins is about the size of a golf ball. One serving of 3 ounces (85g) of chicken is about the size of a deck of cards.

Regular physical activity keeps the body strong while burning the calories absorbed from food.

Regular Physical Activity

Another important part of managing a healthy weight is being active. Regular physical activity keeps the body and

muscles strong, while burning calories for energy. The more physical activity a person does, the more calories his or her body will burn for energy. While cutting calories may be important to initially lose weight, physical activity is an important part of maintaining a healthy weight.

The amount of physical activity needed to maintain a healthy weight varies from person to person. In 2008 the Department of Health and Human Services issued Physical Activity Guidelines for Americans. These guidelines apply to children over six years old, teens, and adults. Under these guidelines, children and teens aged six to seventeen should be physically active for at least sixty minutes per day. This can be broken into shorter segments throughout the day. Playing basketball, walking to school, and taking the stairs all count toward the daily goal. Most of the sixty minutes should be moderate-intensity or vigorous-intensity aerobic physical activity. In addition, the guidelines recommend that as part of their physical activity, children and teens do muscle-strengthening activities such as push-ups and bone strengthening activities such as jumping rope at least three days per week.

Losing weight and keeping it off is not a short-term project. It is a lifetime commitment. Quick fixes, fad diets, and other shortcuts may help a teen drop a few pounds quickly. Yet these methods can deprive a teen's growing body of essential nutrients. They do not teach a teen how to maintain weight loss and live a lifetime at a healthy weight. Instead of shortcuts, health professionals recommend that teens adopt a variety of healthy habits that will help them achieve and maintain a healthy weight.

CHAPTER 3

Weight Loss Controversies— Fad Diets, Pills, and Surgery

F or many people, it is difficult to lose more than a few pounds, and for those who succeed, few are able to maintain their initial weight loss for a long period. Because losing weight and keeping it off is so difficult, many people turn to controversial weight loss methods hoping for a quick and easy solution. Fad diets and diet pills promise quick and easy weight loss but carry other health risks. More invasive methods, such as weight loss surgery can have dramatic results but can also be life threatening.

For teens the allure of quick and easy weight loss may be tempting. Registered dietitian Kristi King explains:

Teens like results that are instantaneous, therefore, [they] tend to go to extremes in order to lose the weight, whether it be cutting back drastically on meals, eliminating certain food groups, turning to weight loss pills and or supplements. All of these things can be very harmful to a growing teenager— so it is best to get sound healthy advice and do it the right way, so that it can be not just a diet but a healthy lifestyle change that can be sustained for an extended period of time.[22]

The Allure of Quick Weight Loss

Most people who have tried to lose weight have been on at least one fad diet. According to the American Academy of Family Physicians, a fad diet is a diet plan that promises dramatic weight loss in a short time. Magazines, newspapers, books, and television commercials strongly promote these diets, promising quick weight loss with little effort. Celebrities who lose weight on fad diets further increase these diets' appeal to teens.

Magazines, newspapers, books, and television commercials strongly promote fad diets—weight loss programs that promise dramatic weight loss over a short time.

Weight Loss Ads: Too Good to Be True

There is no magic drug that can melt away fat. Yet many companies advertise products that they claim can help people lose weight without effort. According to the Federal Trade Commission (FTC), misleading weight loss ads encourage consumers to spend billions of dollars each year. The FTC advises that there are red flags in weight loss ads that can serve to warn consumers that the product is too good to be true. According to the FTC, when looking at a weight loss ad, teens should ask themselves: Does the product claim to

- cause weight loss of 2 pounds (907g) or more a week for a month or more without diet or exercise?
- cause substantial weight loss no matter what or how much a person eats?
- cause permanent weight loss even after stopping using the product?
- block the absorption of fat or calories to enable users to lose substantial weight?
- safely enable consumers to lose more than 3 pounds (1.4kg) per week for more than four weeks?
- cause substantial weight loss for all users?
- cause substantial weight loss by wearing it on the body or rubbing it into the skin?

If the answer is yes, then the weight loss advertising's promises may be too good to be true.

The core of many fad diets is the restriction or elimination of certain food groups. As a result, these plans often lack variety. The restrictions make them very difficult to follow for a long period. Moreover, once people stop following the diet, they often return to their pre-diet eating habits and gain back most of the lost weight. Severe food and calorie restriction can also cause the body's metabolism, the rate at which the body converts food to energy, to slow. With a slower metabolism, the body uses fewer calories to fuel basic functions. After following a fad diet, some people even end up weighing more than they did when they started the diet. "Fad diets may work in the short term, but they are extremely difficult to keep up over time," says King. "In fact, fad diets tend to lead to yo-yo type weight effect, meaning you lose weight—metabolism is altered—

when you go off the fad diet you find yourself regaining weight plus more!"[23]

Popular Fad Diets

At any given time, several fad diet plans are popular among people trying to lose weight. Some plans, like the Atkins or Zone diets, restrict certain types of food. The Atkins diet is one of the most well known fad diets. It was developed by Robert Atkins in the 1970s. The diet emphasizes eating protein-rich foods and severely restricts carbohydrates, particularly during the early stages. By eliminating carbohydrates, the dieter's body goes into ketosis, where the body begins to burn fat because it thinks that it is being starved. In the initial weeks of the diet, weight loss can be very rapid. Yet the Atkins diet can have many negative effects on the body. The severe restriction of carbohydrates may result in side effects that include dizziness, nausea, headaches, and bad breath. According to David L. Katz, director of the Prevention Research Center at the Yale University School of Medicine, the diet "achieves its results by restricting calories, as do all fad diets. People can attain rapid weight loss and lower cholesterol by eliminating any entire food category from their diets, but that doesn't mean it's good for them. Serious illness such as AIDS and cancer tend to cause weight and cholesterol to plummet, but clearly these are not desirable for health."[24]

Other popular fad diets include the Zone diet, which is a diet plan that allows 40 percent of calories from carbohydrates and 30 percent of calories each from protein and fat. Although many people experience rapid weight loss at the beginning, health professionals note that this is usually water loss. The Ornish diet severely limits dietary fat, allowing 10 percent fat, 20 percent protein, and 70 percent carbohydrates. Because the Ornish diet is vegetarian, food choices are mainly whole grains, legumes, fruits, and vegetables. Because the diet is so restrictive, health professionals warn that many people will find it difficult to follow for a long time.

Juice fasts and liquid commercial cleanses promise to detoxify the body, eliminate harmful toxins, and give vital organs a rest. Yet most health professionals point out that healthy kidneys, liver, and bladder do not need help ridding

HEALTH FACT

About two-thirds of dieters regained more weight within four or five years than they initially lost.

the body of toxins. In fact, the beverages in juice fasts and cleanse diets can lead to other health problems because they are often high in refined sugar, which can trigger hunger and blood sugar spikes. The drinks are also often low in protein, an essential nutrient during weight loss because it helps to maintain lean muscle mass and regulate blood sugar and metabolism.

Other fad diet plans have dieters eat one type of food. For example, on the cabbage soup diet, dieters eat mainly homemade cabbage soup. This type of fad diet may result in short-term weight loss because it severely restricts calories. Over the long term however, food-specific diets are extremely difficult to follow. "When you do one of those brand-name diet plans, you're no longer focusing on improving your lifestyle," says Laurie Mitan, an associate professor at Cincinnati Children's Hospital Medical Center in Ohio. "Any pounds you might lose will come back, because you can't stay on those kinds of diets for the rest of your life—it's not healthy or sustainable."[25]

Despite the restrictions, fad diets remain popular across America. Many fad diets deliver quick, short-term weight loss. "Most individuals want cutting-edge solutions for weight loss, and fad diets offer, at least on the surface, 'new' ways to beat the boring mathematical reality of long-term weight loss,"[26] says Robin Steagall, nutrition communications manager for the Calorie Control Council.

Health Risks of Fad Diets

While fad diets may lead to short-term weight loss, they often carry health risks. Because most fad diets are extremely restrictive, they do not provide the minerals and vitamins the body needs to be healthy. Severely restricting calories and nutrients can make a person feel tired, jittery, or moody. Lack of nutrients can also lead to health problems such as anemia (a decrease in healthy red blood cells that carry necessary oxygen to the body's tissues) and osteoporosis (a weakening of the bones to the point that they easily break).

Over time, a highly restricted-calorie diet can slow metabolism, making it harder for the body to burn calories. Some signs that fad diets are not healthy include muscle cramps, dizziness, confusion, fainting, dehydration, severe constipation or diarrhea, and mood changes. Terry Martin, director of the University of California–San Diego's wellness programs, says that with high-protein, low-carbohydrate fad diets, much of the weight loss is actually water loss. The water loss puts increased stress on the kidneys and may lead to various metabolic diseases. "It's futile for most people to sustain it," Martin says. "Over a long period of time, it's hard on your body."[27]

In high protein, low carbohydrate diets much of the weight loss is water, which can strain the kidneys and lead to various metabolic diseases.

For teens, restricting food over a long period during a time of critical growth and development can stunt growth and delay puberty. Because the risks to teens are serious,

most health professionals caution teens against following fad diets. "Fad diets do not work. Fad diets may produce weight loss, but it is often water weight that comes back when normal eating is resumed. Going on extreme diets or fad diets can actually decrease metabolism, which makes it harder to lose weight,"[28] says Haley Lacey, a registered dietitian.

Instead of following fad diets, most health professionals recommend teens follow an overall healthy lifestyle plan that includes long-term healthy eating and regular exercise. "People should follow recommendations made by reputable organizations, such as the Dietary Guidelines for Americans,"[29]

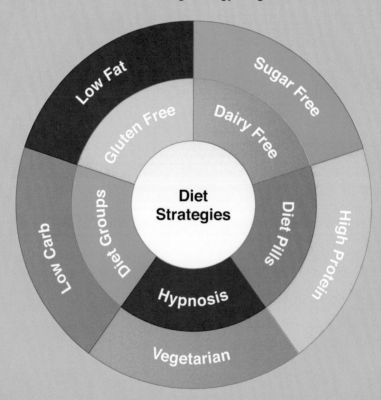

Weight Loss Strategies

One must determine which dieting strategy is right for oneself.

Diet Strategies

Low Fat
Sugar Free
Gluten Free
Dairy Free
Diet Groups
Diet Pills
Low Carb
High Protein
Hypnosis
Vegetarian

says Allen Knehans, chair of the Department of Nutritional Sciences at the University of Oklahoma Health Sciences Center in Oklahoma City. For the long term, healthy eating habits will be more effective than fad diets for maintaining a healthy weight. "Teens should look for something that is moderate and is about lifestyle change. If you don't think you could eat that way for the rest of your life and be happy, avoid it. It is the classic case of the rabbit vs. the turtle—slow and steady wins this race,"[30] says Rebecca Clegg, a licensed professional counselor who specializes in helping clients overcome unhealthy eating patterns.

Weight Loss Supplements

In addition to fad diets, some teens use weight loss supplements that are sold over the counter in grocery stores, drugstores, and health food stores. These products promise to boost metabolism, which makes the body burn more calories for fuel, and melt fat away. Dietary supplements are not subject to the same standards as prescription medications. They can be sold with limited proof of effectiveness or safety. Once a supplement is being sold on the market, however, the U.S. Food and Drug Administration (FDA) can monitor its safety record. If the product proves to be dangerous, the FDA may issue a ban or recall on it.

Many health professionals say that using weight loss supplements is a bad idea for both teens and adults. Many supplements have been linked to harmful and potentially fatal side effects. In 2009 the FDA discovered that sixty-nine different over-the-counter weight loss supplements secretly included pharmaceutical ingredients that could cause serious health complications such as seizures and strokes. Also in 2009, fourteen products from Hydroxycut, one of the top sellers of weight loss supplements, were recalled because of user reports of liver failure and heart problems. "I saw a patient who was taking Hydroxycut and another medication at the same time, and the patient came to the hospital with jaundice and hepatitis," says Ann Scheimann, a pediatric gastroenterologist at Johns Hopkins Children's Center in Baltimore, Maryland. "Dietary supplements aren't regulated.

When you buy them, you're taking a risk."[31] (Hepatitis is inflammation of the liver; jaundice, a yellowing of eyes and skin, is one of the symptoms of hepatitis.) In addition, Scheimann warns that diet pills and supplements can also have a diuretic effect on the body (an increase in urination) that can cause fluid loss and disturb electrolyte levels.

Supplements that claim to boost metabolism and burn more fat can increase blood pressure and heart rate to dangerous levels. "Even in the short term, the potential effects of increased blood pressure and heart rate are stroke and cardiac ischemia, which is when blood stops flowing to the heart muscle," warns Mitan. "We've had teens hospitalized in our ICU [intensive-care unit] with cardiac ischemia after using diet pills just one time!"[32]

Popping Pills: Weight Loss Drugs

Looking for a quick way to lose weight, some adults and teens turn to diet pills to shortcut the hard work of healthy eating and regular exercise. Eighth grader Michael Crandall of North Fort Myers, Florida, wanted to lose weight to increase his chances of making the high school football team. "I want to lose 20 pounds in like 2 months, and I think my long term goal is 50 pounds," Crandall said. He tried diet and exercise before considering diet pills. "At the mall, I would see this stand . . . it's this new teen weight loss pill,"[33] he said. Although Crandall eventually decided not to use the pills and instead stuck with his regimen of diet and exercise, many other teens try weight loss medications.

Just as the use of prescription drugs to manage the condition of people with chronic conditions such as diabetes is appropriate and effective, weight loss drugs may similarly be appropriate for obese adults. Health professionals often categorize adults with a BMI of 30 or above with no obesity-related health conditions and adults with a BMI of 27 to 29.9 with weight-related conditions such as diabetes or high blood pressure as appropriate candidates to use weight loss drugs.

Some weight loss drugs work by suppressing appetite. Appetite suppressants trick the body into thinking that it is not hungry. To do this, appetite suppressants increase serotonin or catecholamine, brain chemicals that affect mood

and appetite. Appetite suppressant medications release medication over a period of time in the body.

Fat absorption inhibitors are another type of weight loss drug. These drugs work by preventing the body from breaking down and absorbing fats in food. Xenical is a fat absorption inhibitor approved for use in the United States. It blocks about 30 percent of dietary fat from being absorbed. Studies show that Xenical is moderately effective and users experience an average weight loss of 12 to 13 pounds (5.4kg to 5.9kg) in one year.

Over the short term, weight loss drugs may improve health in some adults by reducing their risk of weight-related chronic conditions. However, weight loss drugs do have risks associated with use. Side effects can include increased heart rate and blood pressure, sweating, constipation, insomnia,

Many health experts believe that using weight loss supplements is a bad idea for teens and adults because such supplements have been linked to harmful and potentially fatal side effects.

excessive thirst, dizziness, and headache. For fat absorption inhibitors, side effects include excess gas, oily or fatty stools, and oily spotting. In addition, many weight loss drugs appear to lose their effectiveness after about six months of use. Prescription weight loss drugs are controlled substances and can potentially be addictive.

Diet Pills and Teens

When a teen is extremely overweight or obese, losing even a few pounds can improve his or her emotional and physical health. Losing 5 to 7 percent of body weight reduces the risk of weight-related conditions for an overweight or obese person such as type 2 diabetes, cardiovascular disease, and hypertension. Some people believe that weight loss drugs, when managed appropriately and used under a doctor's supervision, can be an effective tool for teen weight management for obese teens.

In 2003 Xenical became the first weight loss drug approved for use by adolescents aged twelve to sixteen.

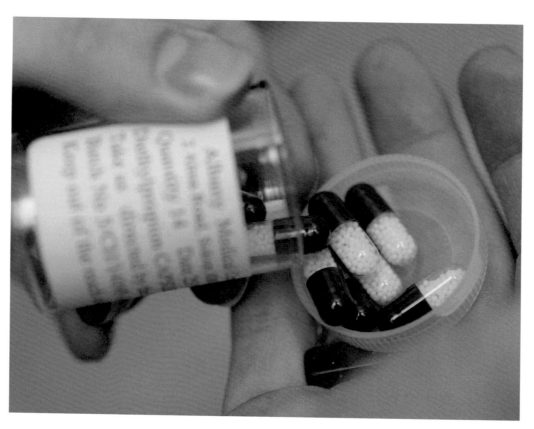

In 2003 Xenical became the first weight loss drug approved for use by adolescents aged twelve to sixteen. Research conducted by Jean-Pierre Chanoine, from the British Columbia Children's Hospital in Vancouver, found that treatment with Xenical, combined with a low-calorie diet, exercise, and behavior therapy, significantly improved weight management for obese teenagers. Teens in the study who used Xenical had an average BMI decrease of 0.55, compared with a 0.31 BMI increase in the control group of teens who did not use the drug.

Many critics of this type of treatment say that teens should not use diet drugs under any circumstances. According to the American Academy of Pediatrics, no over-the-counter weight loss drug has been proved safe and effective for teenagers. "If there was an easy way to do it, I'd know about it," pediatrician Annette MacKoul says. "That's the hard thing to relay to the kids, that yes, you can lose weight quickly, but what's going to happen when you stop those pills?"[34] The National Youth Anti-Drug Media Campaign also has concerns that the stimulants in diet pills could put teens at risk of dependency.

Going Under the Knife: Weight Loss Surgery

In extreme cases some severely obese teens are going under the knife to help them lose weight. Fifteen-year-old Kallum Shropshire from LaFayette, Georgia, made the decision to have surgery after he tried more traditional ways to lose weight and failed. "I've tried dieting and Slim Fast [diet foods], and other fitness programs too," Shropshire says. "It was just a bunch of work that didn't really pay off." Before the surgery, Shropshire weighed more than 400 pounds (181kg). His weight was affecting his health and interfering with activities he enjoyed. "The risk of surgery didn't really matter to me because I really needed something done," he says. "Because I wasn't me, I couldn't really be myself in

> **HEALTH FACT**
>
> The typical American dieter makes four weight loss attempts a year.

front of everybody. I just felt like I was an outcast."[35] In June 2010 Shropshire underwent a gastric sleeve operation that removed about 85 percent of his stomach. Less than four months later, he had dropped 60 pounds (27kg) and hoped to lose another 110 pounds (50kg) in order to reach his goal weight of 250 pounds (113kg).

Bariatric surgery like Shropshire's procedure has become a popular weight loss option for obese adults. Each year between 200,000 and 250,000 obese American adults have bariatric surgery. In the operating room, surgeons use one of several techniques that include gastric bypass, gastric banding, or sleeve gastrectomy to shrink the stomach surgically. Presurgery, the stomach can hold about 1 gallon (3.8L), while after surgery it holds as little as 1 cup (237mL). As a result of their shrunken stomachs, patients feel full faster after surgery. They eat less and lose weight at a fast pace. When gastric bypass is performed, the tiny stomach bypasses part of the small intestine, which reduces the number of calories and nutrients absorbed into the body.

Many adult patients credit the surgery for allowing them to lose significant amounts of weight, 100 pounds (45kg) or more. This has a profound impact on their lives, allowing them to participate more fully in daily life and reducing many chronic health conditions related to obesity, such as heart disease and diabetes. "Before I got my surgery, I was on three different blood pressure medications, two different agents for cholesterol. I took all sorts of medications for aches and pains. I was headed right to diabetes," says fifty-nine-year-old Cathy LaPlant of Shawnee, Kansas. In the three years since her surgery, LaPlant has lost almost 150 pounds (68kg). She no longer needs medications to manage her cholesterol and blood pressure. "It is a wonderful gift," she says. "It is a new chance to do it right this time around. . . . I can bound up steps."[36]

Yet bariatric surgery is not without risks. Like any operation, it can cause serious complications, including infection, leaks, respiratory arrest, and blood clots. In rare cases it can result in death, with a death rate in adult patients of about 0.05 percent for gastric band surgeries and about 0.1 percent for bypass surgeries. Serious complications such as stomach leakage (after gastric bypass and sleeve gastrectomy) and malfunctioning gastric bands can require additional, corrective surgeries.

To date, the FDA has not approved bariatric surgery for adolescents. Although it is not FDA approved, performing gastric surgery on teens is not prohibited, and hospitals across the country admit teenage patients for the procedure. About 1 to 2 percent of all bariatric surgeries are performed on patients under age twenty-one. The maker of the Lap-Band, a device used in gastric banding procedures, is seeking permission from the FDA to market the procedure to patients as young as fourteen.

Bariatric surgery is a popular weight loss option for adults, but many question whether such surgery is the right choice for obese teens because their bodies are still developing.

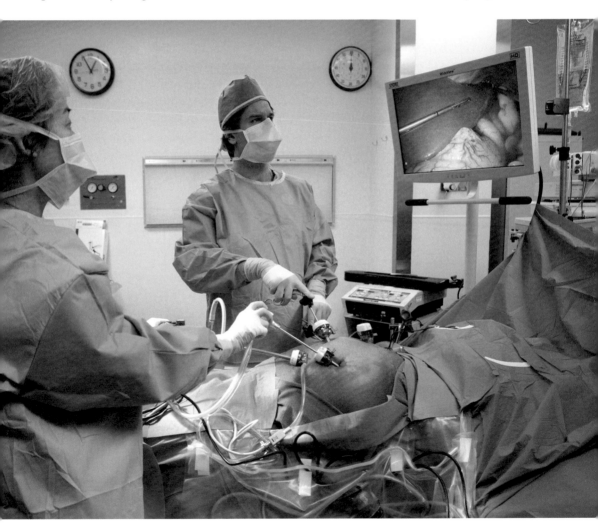

Weight Loss Camps

Some teens are using their summer vacations to lose weight. Unlike "fat camps" where teens are subjected to an extremely rigid schedule and diet, weight loss camps feature fun activities and counseling to help overweight teens learn how to achieve a healthy weight. A good summer weight loss camp will help a teen address self-esteem and body image issues as well as work to lose weight. Teens learn to enjoy healthy and nutritious foods that they can continue to eat long after the camp has ended.

Fourteen-year-old Zarea Adams from Stone Mountain, Georgia, has lost at least 40 pounds (18kg) since attending a local weight loss camp. Before camp Adams was overweight and had a family history of diabetes. Today Adams knows how to read nutrition labels, teaches a Zumba dance fitness class, and encourages her friends to make healthy choices. "Not only does it teach you how to be health conscious, it taught me how to be a better leader," says Adams.

Quoted in Leslie Johnson. "Teen Learns to Live 'Strong,' Lead." *Stone Mountain-Lithonia (GA) Patch*, May 14, 2012. http://stonemountain.patch.com/articles/teen-learns-to-live-strong-lead.

Many people question whether surgery is the right choice for adolescents and teens, whose bodies are still developing. Some health professionals are concerned that weight loss surgery may cause malnutrition in teens, particularly in patients who have gastric bypass, because their shortened small intestine absorbs fewer nutrients. Malnutrition can affect a teen's physical development, including bone growth and reproductive maturation. "Kids across the country are getting this surgery, and we need to know the consequences,"[37] says Mary Horlick, project scientist for the National Institutes of Health, which is sponsoring a study of bariatric surgery in about 250 teenagers.

Despite safety concerns, recent studies support the effectiveness of gastric surgery on teens. A study reported in the

International Journal of Obesity in 2012 found that teenagers with severe obesity can benefit from gastric bypass surgery as much as adults can. Swedish researchers followed eighty-one teens from thirteen to eighteen years old who had undergone gastric bypass surgery. The study subjects lost an average of 96.8 pounds after surgery, which significantly improved their health and quality of life. Torsten Olbers, senior surgeon at Sahlgrenska University Hospital in Sweden and the leader of the study, notes:

> The results are surprisingly good. We will certainly want to carefully examine potential adverse effects of gastric bypass surgery in teenagers. But no other treatment is currently available for this group. Moreover, we know from earlier studies that teenagers with severe obesity are at risk of developing other diseases and poorer quality of life as adults. For that reason, we hope that the method can eventually be offered to more teenagers.[38]

Not a Quick Fix

For teens and adults, the decision to have weight loss surgery should be taken seriously. Doctors caution patients that the surgery is not a magic fix that will take away all of their weight issues. Multiple follow-ups with doctors are required in the first year. After surgery, patients need to learn new healthy eating strategies and develop regular exercise plans. Otherwise, the weight can be gained back, which happens in about 15 percent of adult patients.

Patients also have to pay particular attention to getting adequate nutrition, because gastric surgery can limit the amount of food they can eat. "You really have to learn the difference between listening to your stomach and listening to your head," says Michelle Montanti, a nineteen-year-old bariatric surgery patient. "You have to retrain your body how to eat."[39] Because gastric bypass patients have a higher risk of malnutrition after surgery, taking vitamins and mineral supplements is critical. "If bypass patients stop taking multivitamins, it can result in life-threatening malnutrition,"[40] says Evan Nadler, director of bariatric surgery and codirector of the Obesity Institute at the Children's National Medical Center, in Washington, D.C.

Despite the risks, some people see weight loss surgery as a potentially lifesaving treatment for extremely obese teens. "Bariatric surgery is increasingly becoming a treatment option for adolescents, and in the right setting and with proper evaluation, it may be appropriate,"[41] says Daniel A. DeUgart, a pediatric surgeon at the University of California–Los Angeles.

CHAPTER 4

Weight Loss Gone Wrong

When Tish Lindberg was in the seventh grade, she was self-conscious about being overweight. She decided to diet to lose a few pounds. Her focus on weight quickly turned into an unhealthy obsession. "I decided I got tired of depriving myself and started eating and throwing up," she says. Lindberg developed an eating disorder called bulimia nervosa, in which a person binge eats and then purges by vomiting, using laxatives, or other similar methods to get rid of the food. "I'd cook pancakes for several hours, eat them and purge and go back and eat more,"[42] says Lindberg.

Many people struggle with their weight. For some like Lindberg, an unhealthy focus on weight can become an obsession that leads to significant mental, emotional, and physical problems. In some cases weight obsession can lead to life-threatening eating disorders. A focus on "weight loss for teens is not very safe, as teens are at high risk of developing eating disorders,"[43] says Jessica Setnick, a registered dietitian.

The Downside of Dieting

According to the CDC, approximately 69 percent of Americans are overweight or obese. According to the CDC's 2011

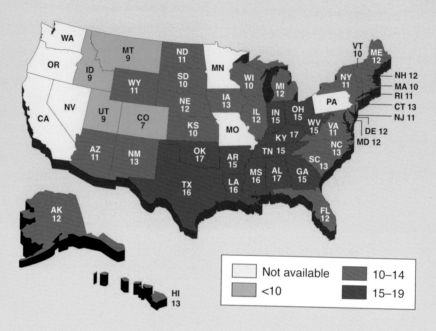

CDC Youth Risk Behavior Survey, 2011 Percentage of Obese Students

WA
OR
ID 9
MT 9
ND 11
MN
SD 10
WY 11
NE 12
IA 13
WI 10
MI 12
NY 11
VT 10
ME 12
NH 12
MA 10
RI 11
CT 13
NJ 11
NV
UT 9
CO 7
KS 10
MO
IL 12
IN 15
OH 15
PA
CA
AZ 11
NM 13
OK 17
AR 15
KY 17
WV 15
VA 11
TN 15
NC 13
SC 13
DE 12
MD 12
MS 16
AL 17
GA 15
TX 16
LA 16
AK 12
FL 12
HI 13

Not available
<10
10–14
15–19

Taken from: Centers for Disease Control and Prevention. www.cdc.gov/healthyyouth/obesity/obesity-youth.htm.

National Youth Risk Behavior Survey, about 13 percent of high school students are obese and 15 percent are overweight. To lose weight, many people go on a diet. According to the National Eating Disorders Association, 45 percent of women and 25 percent of men are on a diet on any given day. The pressure to diet to be thin affects teens as well, with 46 percent of teens reporting in the 2011 CDC survey that they were trying to lose weight.

Although some dieters are successful, the majority are not. According to Dianne Neumark-Sztainer, a researcher and professor at the School of Public Health at the University of Minnesota, diets often fail because people treat them as a short-term project. "Dieting is typically viewed as a temporary behavior," she says. "It is often viewed as a project. But for long-term weight change and maintenance, ongoing lifestyle changes that allow for some flexibility are needed."[44]

Many diets fail because they rely on rigid rules for short-term success. Rules about eating foster feelings of deprivation, which can cause a dieter to binge on forbidden foods. When the dieter resolves again to follow strict diet rules, a vicious cycle of dieting and bingeing can develop. Over time, this cycle can actually lead to weight gain instead of weight loss. "Dieting is a terrible idea for anyone, teens or adults. It causes deprivation, which then causes overeating. We all know people who weight cycle—lose a bunch of weight, gain it back, lose it, gain it. It's extremely unhealthy and hard on self-esteem as well,"[45] says Setnick.

In addition, some teens resort to unhealthy behaviors when they decide to lose weight. According to the CDC, one in ten American teens uses unhealthy behaviors to lose weight. These behaviors include going without eating for twenty-four hours or more, taking diet pills or laxatives, or forcing themselves to vomit. Health professionals warn that these unhealthy behaviors in teens can lead to medical problems caused by a lack of nutrients during critical growth years. "Often times, once teens begin to experiment with these behaviors, it can be difficult to get out of the habit of them, especially if they receive positive feedback from peers and others about the initial weight loss," explains Ginger Hartman, a registered dietitian at Eating Recovery Centers Behavioral Hospital for Children and Adolescents in Denver, Colorado. "These types of comments can often influence the teen to continue the behaviors and/or increase the frequency of behaviors. Eventually, the teen may no longer be able to control the behaviors and may find him or herself struggling with a life-threatening eating disorder."[46]

Weight Obsession

For thousands of people, dieting becomes more than an attempt to lose a few pounds. It becomes an unhealthy obsession. Teens with a weight obsession may become fixated on how much they weigh, instead of focusing on being healthy and strong. They may obsessively count every calorie and set severe rules and restrictions about eating. They may eat only one type of food or skip entire meals to drink only water or chew gum. They may compulsively exercise and feel guilty if they miss a single workout.

Weight-obsessed teens often fixate on the scale and weigh themselves repeatedly, sometimes multiple times per day. Body weight normally fluctuates throughout the day. Most health professionals suggest that people weigh themselves once a week at the same time of day as part of a healthy weight management program. Teens who weigh themselves more than once a day could be too focused on the scale's reading and may not get an accurate picture of true health. "The focus should be on overall health, not on reaching a number on a scale,"[47] says registered dietitian Haley Lacey.

What Is an Eating Disorder?

In some cases an unhealthy obsession with weight can lead to a more serious problem, an eating disorder. Eating disorders such as anorexia, bulimia, and binge eating disorder are complex and serious illnesses. People with eating disorders are generally obsessed with food, weight, and appearance. "Usually kids with eating disorders spend a good portion of their day worrying about food, weight, and their body size, while other kids tend to be less obsessive,"[48] says Kerri Boutelle, a weight and eating disorders expert at the University of Minnesota.

Eating disorders are a widespread problem. According to the National Eating Disorders Association, as many as 10 million females and 1 million males in the United States have an eating disorder such as anorexia or bulimia. Millions more struggle with a binge eating disorder. While eating disorders most commonly affect young women, they can strike both genders and affect people of all ages, social classes, and races.

An eating disorder appears as a severe disturbance in eating behaviors

HEALTH FACT

Anorexia is the third-most common chronic illness among adolescents.

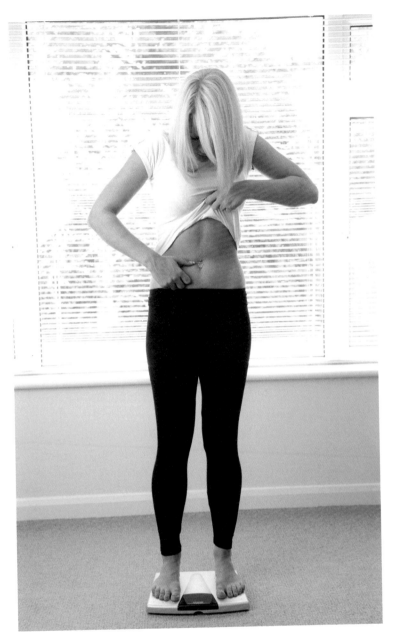

and how a person thinks about food and body image. People with eating disorders may restrict the food they eat, binge eat, force themselves to vomit, take laxatives, or compulsively exercise. Symptoms of eating disorders include extreme emotions, attitudes, and behaviors about weight and food as well as physical problems that can affect daily activities and personal relationships. If allowed to spiral out of control, eating disorders can result in death. Kathryn J. Zerbe, a professor of psychiatry at Oregon Health and Science University, explains:

> Eating disorders should be thought of as a spectrum. The occasional pizza or ice cream splurge with friends does not make you a binge eater. The specific diagnosis of anorexia nervosa, bulimia nervosa or atypical eating disorder must be rendered when the pursuit of thinness becomes more entrenched, ascetic [strict] restriction of food worsens, or when binge and purge cycles become more frequent and when the preoccupation with body image grows more distorted.[49]

Many times, an eating disorder develops as the result of another underlying psychological problem. A person may be trying to deal with emotional pain, low self-esteem, depression, lack of control, or stress. According to the National Eating Disorders Association:

> While eating disorders may begin with preoccupations with food and weight, they are most often about much more than food. People with eating disorders use food and the control of food in an attempt to compensate for feelings and emotions that may otherwise seem overwhelming. For some, dieting, bingeing, and purging may begin as a way to cope with painful emotions and to feel in control of one's life.[50]

Anorexia Nervosa

Anorexia nervosa is a serious, potentially life-threatening eating disorder. The most obvious symptom is low body weight, at least 15 percent below ideal body weight. People with anorexia are obsessed with food, weight, and being thin. They have an intense fear of gaining weight, coupled with a distorted body image and a denial of how serious their illness is. This can lead to emotional, mental, and physical problems. Like other eating disorders, anorexia is considered a mental illness. It is also a medical illness that usually results

Warning Signs of an Eating Disorder

The first warning signs of an eating disorder often involve a teen's behaviors around food. A teen with an eating disorder may regularly skip meals, eat only small amounts of food, or restrict his or her intake to only low-calorie foods. Some teens may give excuses to avoid eating in public. Others may hide or throw away food to avoid consuming it. Some resort to purging, or forcing themselves to vomit, to get rid of food in their body.

How a teen views his or her body may also be a warning sign of an eating disorder. If teens insist that they are fat when they are not, appear disgusted by their body and shape, or wear big clothes to hide how much weight they are losing, they may have an eating disorder. When teens begin to exercise obsessively to the point of exhaustion, trying to burn calories even though they are eating very little, it may also be a warning sign.

Imbalances, extremes, or fixations within a teen's thoughts and emotions can also be warning signs of an eating disorder. Many people with eating disorders believe that being thin will fix all problems in their life. They are convinced that losing a few pounds will make them happier, more successful, or more lovable. When they fail on a diet, they may feel guilty, unworthy, hopeless, powerless, or unloved.

Teens with an eating disorder may regularly skip meals, eat only very small amounts, or restrict their intake to only one, low-calorie food.

from a person trying to use food and body weight to control other problems.

Although it can strike men and women of all ages, anorexia most commonly develops in adolescent girls and young adult women. According to the National Alliance on Mental Illness, 0.5 to 1 percent of females in the United States develop anorexia. More than 90 percent of those affected are adolescent and young women.

People with anorexia nervosa are obsessed with their weight and body image, and have such a distorted view of their bodies that they continue to try to get thinner.

People with anorexia maintain their low body weight by restricting the food they eat. Many restrict calories to fewer than one thousand per day. Often, people with anorexia regularly skip entire meals. They may stay away from situations in which they would be expected to eat. They find ways to hide food and trick others into believing that they have eaten, and they make excuses for when they are not eating. When they do eat, people with anorexia may consume only low-fat, low-calorie foods and beverages such as lettuce, celery, popcorn, and diet sodas.

As the illness progresses, people with anorexia may develop ritualistic eating habits such as cutting their food into tiny pieces or fixing elaborate meals for others that they do not eat themselves. Food and weight become an increasing obsession and take over much of their thoughts. The act of eating can become repulsive or frightening to people suffering from anorexia. After they do eat, some force themselves to throw up. Others may exercise for long periods of time to burn calories. Over time, these behaviors become increasingly difficult to stop. "Once someone starts down the slippery slope of starvation, it simply spins out of control," says Cynthia Bulik, director of the UNC Eating Disorders Program at the University of North Carolina–Chapel Hill. "Even if the person wants to recover, it becomes enormously hard to eat and restore weight. The fear and anxiety underlying anorexia nervosa become paralyzing to recovery."[51]

Anorexia can cause serious health problems. Without adequate calories and nutrients, the body cannot function normally. It is forced to slow down basic processes in order to conserve energy. As a result, young women may stop having menstrual periods; hair and nails may become brittle, and skin can turn dry and yellow. Bones lacking calcium may become brittle and break easily. In addition, people with anorexia often feel cold because their body temperature drops. They develop lanugo, soft, fine hair like that on a newborn baby, on their body.

HEALTH FACT

Only one in ten people with an eating disorder receives treatment.

More seriously, starving the body can cause damage to vital organs such as the heart, kidneys, and brain. Pulse and blood pressure decrease, and the cardiovascular system may experience irregular heart rhythms or heart failure. In extreme cases people with anorexia literally starve themselves to death. In fact, anorexia has the highest mortality rate of any psychiatric illness. According to the National Eating Disorders Association, between 5 and 20 percent of people with anorexia will die from the illness.

Bulimia Nervosa

Bulimia nervosa, or bulimia, is an eating disorder that includes cycles of bingeing and purging. A person binges, or eats enormous quantities of food at one time, often so much that his or her stomach hurts. Bingeing is not simply overeating. People who binge feel out of control. They cannot stop the urge to binge once it begins and only stop eating when they are too sick to continue, are interrupted, or run out of food. After bingeing, they feel guilty and purge or use other behaviors to control weight. Often, people with bulimia purge by making themselves vomit. Others abuse laxatives, diuretics, and enemas. In some cases people with bulimia do not purge regularly. Instead, they use other compensatory behaviors such as fasting or excessive exercise to control weight after a binge.

Because of the alternating binges, purges, and fasts, weight fluctuations in people with bulimia are common. Unlike anorexics, who become bony and emaciated, people with bulimia are often of normal weight and are sometimes overweight. For this reason, bulimia is called an invisible eating disorder.

Bulimia typically develops during late adolescence or early adulthood. Like other eating disorders, bulimia primarily affects females. In fact, of those diagnosed with the disorder, approximately 80 percent are female. According to the National Eating Disorders Association, approximately 1 to 2 percent of adolescent and young adult women have bulimia. Bulimia is also linked to anorexia. According to the National Alliance on Mental Illness, approximately 50 percent of people with anorexia will go on to develop bulimia.

Bulimia can cause serious damage to a person's body. The frequent binge-and-purge cycles can harm the digestive system. Purging can also lead to an electrolyte imbalance. Electrolytes are minerals in the body, such as calcium, potassium, and sodium, that have an electric charge. An imbalance of electrolytes can lead to dehydration, affect the heart and other major organs, or disrupt body functions. Frequent vomiting also brings up fluids from the stomach into the esophagus and mouth. The acids in these fluids can cause tooth decay and staining. Frequent vomiting can also cause inflammation and possible rupture of the esophagus, which can be life threatening. In some cases binge eating can cause the stomach to rupture. In addition, purging depletes

Bulimia nervosa is an eating disorder that includes cycling between bingeing and purging.

Jessica's Story

Today Jessica Setnick is a pediatric dietitian in Dallas, Texas. She meets with children and teens to address a variety of weight and eating issues. She also teaches other health professionals how to recognize and help people with eating disorders. Jessica brings firsthand experience to her job because she suffered from bulimia as a teen. Jessica says:

> I always thought I needed to lose weight, and looking back at photos now, I can see that it was my internal sense of myself that was off, not my body size. I developed an eating disorder after following a fad diet. I under ate for a few weeks and then after a while could only control my eating in front of others and then over-ate secretly and forced myself to throw up. It was absolutely awful, and it actually resulted in weight gain.[1]

After struggling for four years with bulimia, Jessica found the strength to take back control of her eating. Yet her experience did have an unforeseen benefit. "I'm grateful that it led me to my calling: counseling others who are fighting the same battle. Originally, I thought that becoming a dietitian would give me the answers to my food and weight problems, but it turns out that overcoming my food and weight problems made me a better dietitian,"[2] she says.

1. Jessica Setnick. E-mail to the author, November 19, 2012.
2. Jessica Setnick. "An RD Confesses: I Had Bulimia." *Fitness*, March 2006. www .fitnessmagazine.com/health/body-image/stories/an-rd-confesses-i-had -bulimia/?page=6.

the body of vital minerals like potassium, which can result in heart failure. "If people are trying to control their weight . . . they can kill themselves if they purge themselves, take laxatives or starve themselves," says Richard Pesikoff, a professor of psychiatry at Baylor College of Medicine in Houston, Texas. "If you vomit up potassium, your potassium levels drop. Then you get cardiac arrhythmia, and multiple vomiting can lead to cardiac arrest and death."[52]

Binge Eating Disorder

Everyone overeats at times, especially on holidays or special occasions. For some people, however, overeating becomes a regular occurrence. Binge eating is the frequent eating of enormous amounts of food even if a person is not hungry. Often done in secret, binge eating is a compulsion. Binge eaters feel as if they cannot resist the urge to gorge and continue eating. Unlike a person with bulimia, a binge eater does not purge food or exercise obsessively to control weight. As a result, most people with binge eating disorders are overweight or obese. According to the National Eating Disorders Association, approximately 1 to 5 percent of the general population suffers from binge eating disorder, with

Binge eating is the consumption of an enormous amount of food at one sitting, even if the person is not hungry.

slightly more women (60 percent) being affected than men (40 percent).

Kelsey is a seventeen-year-old from Philadelphia who is one of hundreds of thousands of teen girls dealing with binge eating disorder. She says:

> A typical binge will go something like this: I tell myself I'm only going to have one cookie, but it turns into ten. After I eat those, I'll grab some chips because I want something salty. Next thing you know, I'm standing in front of the fridge eating leftovers. Then I'll want something sweet again, so I'll have a couple of ice cream sandwiches and some cereal. It's as if I'm on autopilot just shoving all the food in and before I realize it, I've eaten a ton.

Kelsey admits that she is too ashamed to binge eat in front of others, so she waits until she is alone. "When my mom leaves, I sometimes go straight to the kitchen so I can have a huge pig-out with no one around,"[53] she says.

Although no single cause has been linked to binge eating disorder, some health professionals believe that dieting may play a role in triggering it. Overweight people often restrict food when dieting. Depriving themselves of food and calories may trigger a binge eater's urge to gorge on food. "There's only so long that we as humans can deprive ourselves; it's against our nature. So the binge usually comes after the diet, or a big binge is what ends the diet. It's a vicious cycle and very hard to stop,"[54] says Amy Jaffe, a nutrition therapist in Coral Gables, Florida.

Boys and Eating Disorders

Although teen girls are more likely to develop eating disorders, teen boys can also be affected by anorexia, bulimia, and other eating disorders. The symptoms of eating disorders in males are similar to those in females. They include an unhealthy obsession with food, weight, and body image, excessive restriction of calories, bingeing, and purging.

Eric Ostendorf's anorexia began when he was ten years old and realized that he was not as athletic as his friends were and was a little overweight. One day after glancing at his dad's fitness magazine, he started doing sit-ups. Gradually, he cut out carbohydrates from his diet and ate lean protein such as chicken breasts and egg whites. His workouts grew longer until he was running about 7 to 8 miles (11km to 13km), lifting weights for an hour, playing soccer for two hours, and doing abdominal exercises every day. As a result of his compulsive exercising and eating restrictions, Eric's weight dropped to 79 pounds (36kg). "My body was a machine," Eric says. "It was just exercising. . . . I never felt tired because I never let my mind register that I was tired."[55] Even after he was hospitalized at age fifteen for a dangerously low heart rate, Eric did not stop exercising and dieting.

Eventually, Eric realized that he needed help and agreed to go to a residential treatment program for eating disorders. In the program, Eric was surrounded by other male eating disorder patients who helped him recognize the extent of his eating disorder. He says that his health was so bad, he was two weeks away from a heart attack. "This was my last chance to get help with this," he says. "At this point, I realized how much it affected my parents, myself."[56] Although it was difficult, Eric learned to let go of his anorexia and exercise obsession. Today, he hopes to go to medical school so that he can treat children and teens with eating disorders.

CHAPTER **5**

Living at a Healthy Weight

Making healthy choices about food and physical activity can improve how a person feels and performs physically and mentally. Fresh foods such as fruits, vegetables, lean meats, and low-fat dairy are nutritionally dense. They cut hunger and make a person feel full longer than empty junk food. Regular physical activity keeps the body functioning optimally and builds strong bones and muscles. Understanding how to create good behaviors around food and make healthy food choices, along with smart exercise, are key components of living at a healthy weight.

Healthy Eating Tips

Living a healthy lifestyle starts with choosing a balanced eating plan. According to the Dietary Guidelines for Americans 2010, a healthy eating plan emphasizes fruits, vegetables, whole grains, and fat-free or low-fat dairy products. It includes lean meats, fish, beans, eggs, and nuts. A healthy eating plan minimizes the amount of saturated fats, trans fats, cholesterol, salt, and added sugars in foods and drinks.

Many teens find that simply choosing to eat more healthful foods can help them achieve and maintain a healthy weight. Some easy steps to healthy eating include eating

A healthy eating plan minimizes the amounts of unhealthy fats, cholesterol, salt, and added sugars in foods and beverages.

fewer fatty foods, downsizing portions, and eating more fruits and vegetables. Nineteen-year-old Rebecca M. has lost about 51 pounds (23kg) over four years by gradually cutting back on fatty foods and giving up chips, fries, full-fat salad dressings, and soda. She explains:

> I gradually started to cut my portions. Then I gradually stopped eating things that were high in fat or calories. It was easier for me to slowly reduce these foods and my portions than just changing everything in one day. I didn't stop eating a Sunday-morning doughnut until about a month and a half after I started my

weight loss plan. Choosing not to eat that doughnut and having a banana instead was just the next step in the process.[57]

According to the CDC, a healthy eating plan includes a variety of foods. Teens should try to focus on the new foods they should eat, instead of thinking about the foods that they should not have. New foods can include mangoes or kiwi and other exotic fruits, grilled vegetables with herbs, and low-fat yogurts. A new food can also be a healthful twist on an old recipe. Instead of frying or breading chicken, a baked or grilled version may taste as good. According to recommendations

Felicia's Story

At age fourteen Felicia Schiel wanted to lose weight. Like many teens, she enjoyed pizza and fast food with her friends after school and spent a lot of time playing video games, texting classmates, and typing at a computer. Schiel noticed that her habits were having an effect on her weight and making breathing difficult. So she decided to change what she ate and increase her activity to return to a healthy weight. "I just kept getting fatter and fatter each year," she explains. She says she realized that "if I didn't do it now; I'd probably be 20 pounds heavier." Schiel began working out with a personal trainer at a local fitness center. The trainer also helped Schiel incorporate more healthy foods into her diet. "Carbs, like oatmeal, are important. I try to get her to eat protein, calcium, fruit and make sure she doesn't skip breakfast and has a little something before she works out. And I tell her that as long as she is eating right all week, she can have one day where she can eat what she wants," says Terese Culver, Schiel's trainer. One year later, Schiel has lost weight, dropped several clothing sizes, and feels healthier. "I feel a lot better now," she says. "I have more energy. And I can walk a lot longer now."

Quoted in "Teen's Decision to Hire Trainer Prompts Weight Loss, Confidence Boost." *Wilkes-Barre (PA) Times Leader*, January 24, 2009.

from the CDC, "Healthy eating is all about balance. You can enjoy your favorite foods even if they are high in calories, fat or added sugars. The key is eating them only once in a while and balance them out with healthier foods and more physical activity."[58]

Education Is Important

If a person does not know the difference between a high-fat burger at a fast food restaurant and a lower-fat salad, then it is difficult to make healthy food choices. Education and understanding the right balance of foods to eat are important. Most experts agree on the following guidelines for healthy eating:

- Eat a variety of foods to get a balanced mix of all the nutrients the body needs.
- Eat more fruits and vegetables and fewer animal products.
- Eat more fresh and homemade foods and fewer processed and packaged foods.
- Cut down on saturated and trans fats, especially those in whole-fat dairy products; fried foods; processed snack foods; and baked goods with trans fats. Unsaturated fats that are part of a healthy diet come from fish and nuts.
- Choose food with complex carbohydrates. Cut down on the simple sugars of sodas and foods made with highly refined white flour. Instead, choose foods that list whole grain as the first ingredient.
- Eat or drink about three cups of nonfat or low-fat dairy products each day. Calcium is especially important in the bone-building teen years.
- Eat protein in moderation. Choose lean proteins like fish and skinless chicken.
- Limit daily sodium intake. Stop adding table salt to foods and cut back on canned, processed foods that are high in salt.

Dietitian Haley Lacey works with children and teens and knows that healthy eating is the foundation of a healthy weight. She tells her patients to eat in moderation and focus on healthy foods. "There are no foods that should be totally off limits," she says. "Fruits and vegetables, lean meats, low fat dairy, and whole grains should be the foundation of a healthy diet. Processed snacks, fast food, candy, and other high calorie foods should be eaten rarely."[59]

Limit Sugary Drinks and Fatty Foods

Teens who have achieved a healthy weight have used many strategies to help them eat well and avoid diet pitfalls. One of the easiest strategies that many teens recommend is to change what they drink. Switching from juice and soda to

Switching from a twenty-ounce regular soda to a twenty-ounce diet soda can save 227 calories, and drinking a glass of water before each meal can help reduce feelings of hunger.

water and other low-calorie beverages can save hundreds of calories per day. For example, switching from a 20-ounce (0.6L) cola to a 20-ounce diet soda or water can save up to 227 calories. In addition, many health experts recommend drinking a glass of water before each meal to help control feelings of hunger.

Cutting fatty foods is another big part of healthy eating. According to the Dietary Guidelines for Americans 2010, the recommended total fat intake for teens up to age eighteen is between 25 and 35 percent of calories. For older teens and adults, the recommended amount is between 20 and 35 percent of calories. For example, a teen who is maintaining his or her weight on two thousand calories per day should be getting between five hundred to seven hundred calories from fat. A gram of fat has more than double the calories (nine) than a gram of carbohydrates (four) or protein (four).

Eating a healthy breakfast is important to jump-start one's metabolism for the day and should include whole grains, proteins, and fruit.

As a result, higher-fat foods are usually more calorie dense than low-fat foods. "I avoid all notoriously fatty foods and greasy ways of preparing foods. I only eat fat-free salad dressing and I never eat mayo,"[60] says teenager Jack F.

Eat Regular Meals

HEALTH FACT

About 24 percent of high school students report drinking at least one soda per day.

Skipping meals, especially breakfast, can sabotage a healthy eating plan. "Hunger can be a powerful trigger to eat and overeat,"[61] says Molly Gee, a dietitian at Baylor College of Medicine in Houston, Texas. She explains that skipping a meal can make a person so hungry that he or she chooses larger portions or the wrong types of foods at the next meal. In order to maintain energy levels throughout the day, Gee recommends eating every four to five hours.

Breakfast in particular is an important meal to start the day. "It's difficult to get in all the necessary nutrients without including breakfast,"[62] says Gee. A healthy breakfast should include whole grains, protein, and fruit. Eating a healthy breakfast can jump-start the metabolism for the day, help a person feel full longer, and make it easier to eat healthfully for the rest of the day.

A study at the University of Minnesota's School of Public Health confirmed the importance for teens of eating a regular breakfast. Researchers in the school's Project EAT (Eating Among Teens) studied more than twenty-two hundred adolescents and the association between breakfast frequency and five-year body weight change. The researchers found that the teens who were daily breakfast eaters tended to gain less weight and have lower BMI levels than those who skipped breakfast. Dianne Neumark-Sztainer, principal investigator of Project EAT, says this research confirms the importance of eating breakfast. "Although adolescents may think that skipping breakfast seems like a good way to save on calories, findings suggest the opposite," she says. "Eating a healthy breakfast may help adolescents avoid overeating later in the day and disrupt unhealthy eating patterns, such as not eating early in the day and eating a lot late in the evening."[63]

Moderation Is Key

Experts warn that one of teens' biggest mistakes is to make extreme changes in hopes of quick weight loss. Kristi King, a registered dietitian specializing in pediatrics and adolescents at Texas Children's Hospital, explains:

> Teens like results that are instantaneous, and tend to go to extremes in order to lose the weight. Whether it be cutting back drastically on meals, eliminating certain food groups, turning to weight loss pills and/ or supplements. All of these things can be very harmful to a growing teenager—so it is best to get sound healthy advice and do it the right way, so that it can be not just a diet but a healthy lifestyle change that can be sustained for an extended period of time.

King recommends moderation and patience for teens working to achieve a healthy weight. "Patience is key. Remember slow and steady wins the race. Stick to it, the results will be worth it in the end,"[64] she says.

Moderation helps teens avoid feelings of deprivation, which can sabotage any weight management plan and lead to bingeing. Many teens who are successful at maintaining a healthy weight say that they do not deny themselves the foods they crave. Instead, they develop strategies that allow them to enjoy smaller portions of those foods within an overall healthy eating plan. They may limit portion sizes, have designated times to eat craved foods, or enjoy lower-calorie versions of favorite treats. "I do get cravings, and I allow myself to indulge. But I always try to keep it down to a minimum—like a piece of chocolate instead of a whole bar or bag, or small-size French fries,"[65] says teen Kristy C.

Family Meals

Families with teenagers know that finding a time for everyone to sit down together to eat a meal can be challenging. However, making time for a family meal can help teens eat more healthfully. As they eat together, parents can model

Empty Calories

Many foods and beverages that teens eat and drink contain empty calories. Empty calories come from solid fats like butter and shortening and/or added sugars and syrups that have very few nutrients. Some solid fats are found naturally in foods, like the fat in a steak. Other solid fats, along with added sugars and syrups, are added during food processing or preparation.

Empty calories can sabotage a healthy diet because they increase a food's calorie count but add few or no nutrients. One simple way to eat more healthfully is to limit empty calories.

Common foods full of empty calories include:

- Cakes, cookies, pastries, and donuts (contain both solid fat and added sugars)
- Sodas, energy drinks, sports drinks, and fruit drinks (contain added sugars)
- Pizza (contains solid fat and is often topped with added unhealthy foods such as pepperoni)
- Ice cream (contains both solid fat and added sugars)
- Sausages, hot dogs, bacon, and ribs (contain solid fat)

Empty-calorie, or junk, food is high in sugar and fat—which provide calories—but is lacking in other needed nutrients.

healthy eating habits and choices for teens. In fact, a 2009 study reported in the *Journal of Nutrition Education and Behavior* found that adolescents who participated in regular family meals reported more healthful diets and meal patterns compared with adolescents who did not participate in regular family meals.

A study by the medical journal Pediatrics *reported that teens who ate at least five meals a week with their families were 35 percent less likely to have an eating disorder than teens who rarely ate meals with their families.*

In addition, gathering for regular family meals can reduce disordered eating in teens. A study reported in the June 2011 issue of *Pediatrics* stated that teens who ate at least five meals a week with their families were 35 percent less likely to engage in disordered eating than teens who did not. In the study, disordered eating behaviors included bingeing and purging, taking diet pills, self-induced vomiting, using laxatives or diruetics, fasting, skipping meals, or smoking cigarettes to lose weight. "For children and adolescents with

disordered eating, mealtime provides a setting in which parents can recognize early signs and take steps to prevent detrimental patterns from turning into full-blow[n] eating disorders,"[66] says Barbara Fiese, a University of Illinois professor of human development and family studies and director of the Family Resiliency Center.

Tips for Eating Out

Restaurant meals can be a pitfall for healthy eating, because many restaurants serve enormous portions that are high in fat and calories. Eating out does not have to be unhealthy. Once again, planning is important. People can ask waiters how food is prepared. Foods that are sautéed or have cream sauces are probably high in fat and calories. Lean, grilled menu items are usually better choices. Some restaurants even offer guides on their menu to show which items are low-fat, heart-healthy, or low-carbohydrate options.

Most fast food restaurants also serve low-fat, low-calorie options. They often have nutrition information available at the restaurant in order to compare menu items. Alternatively, many restaurants post nutrition information on corporate websites. At McDonald's restaurants, a regular hamburger, side salad (without dressing), and apple dippers with caramel dip has only 375 calories and 10 grams of fat. At KFC an original recipe chicken breast (without skin or breading), seasoned rice, and green beans has only 340 calories and 5.5 grams of fat.

Get Moving

Regular exercise is an important tool for keeping weight in a healthy range. "It's not just diet, but exercise too," says King. "You can make healthy food changes and see results, but if you add exercise to that, the results will be more significant."[67] More physical activity burns more calories for energy. Combined with reducing calories through nutritious eating, exercising can lead to achieving a healthy weight. According to the CDC, studies affirm that regular physical activity is the only way to maintain weight loss and live at a healthy weight. In addition, physical activity reduces the risk of chronic illnesses such as cardiovascular disease and diabetes more than weight loss alone.

Health professionals at the Children's Hospital of Pittsburgh Weight Management and Wellness Center recommend that teens spend an hour every day doing some type of physical activity. At least twenty minutes of that time should be vigorous aerobic activity. Physical activity should be fun, and teens should pick something they enjoy, whether it is skiing or a Pilates class. Teens can also increase physical activity by reducing the time they spend doing inactive behaviors such as watching television or playing video games. Instead, simple choices such as walking the family dog or taking the stairs instead of the elevator can increase daily physical activity. Other tips for teens to incorporate physical activity into daily living include planning ahead, tracking progress, trying new activities, joining a sport or enrolling in an exercise class, and spending more time outside.

Teens should also try to vary the type of exercise that they do. Different activities have benefits, and alternating them can reduce boredom. Experts recommend that teens participate in strength and flexibility activities two to three times a week. Examples of these activities include stretching, martial arts, yoga, push-ups, and weight lifting. Teens should also participate in active aerobic activities three to five times per week. These activities include sports like basketball, biking, jogging, rollerblading, swimming, and dancing.

Michelle Williams from British Columbia, Canada, was active in sports in high school, but in college she quit exercising and developed unhealthy eating habits. Two years after graduation, the 5-foot-4-inch Williams weighed close to 200 pounds (91kg). Unhappy with her unhealthy weight, Williams revamped her eating plan and replaced high-fat, high-calorie foods with healthier alternatives. She also joined a gym to increase her physical activity. "My first day there, I could barely walk half a mile, but I just pushed myself to go a little longer and a little

HEALTH FACT

Fourteen percent of adolescents aged thirteen to seventeen skip breakfast regularly.

faster every session,"[68] she says. Steadily, she lost weight and dropped about 35 pounds (16kg) in six months. Encouraged, Williams added weight training to her exercise routine and lost 11 more pounds (5kg) in two months.

Weighing In

Many teens who have successfully maintained a healthy weight have discovered that regular weight checks can help them manage and maintain a healthy weight. Regular weigh-ins can identify small weight gains and give teens

Experts recommend that teens spend an hour every day in some type of physical activity, including twenty minutes of vigorous aerobic activity.

Teens who regularly weigh themselves can address unhealthy weight gain as it arises and take measures to get back on a healthier plan.

the opportunity to make changes in their diet and activity and stop the weight gain before it becomes too large. "I can always tell if my pants have gotten tighter or if I weigh more. Then I know it's time to watch what I eat or work out more,"[69] says teen McKenzie K.

Health experts caution, however, that while regular weight checks can be useful, teens should not go overboard by weighing themselves too frequently. "Don't weigh yourself more than once a week, as daily weights introduce too much natural error such as body fluid fluctuations, and is way too obsessive,"[70] says Jessica Setnick, a registered dietitian who specializes in treating teens and adults with eating disorders.

Kelly's Success Story

Finding and maintaining a healthy weight takes hard work and commitment. For the past two years, fourteen-year-old Kelly Morrison has made healthy choices a part of her daily life. As a child, Morrison was overweight and did not feel comfortable in her own skin. She was sedentary and ate a lot of unhealthy food. At age twelve she met with a dietitian who helped her identify unhealthy behaviors and develop strategies to fix them. Against the advice of her dietitian, Morrison first tried to cut her calories drastically to lose weight. "I cut my caloric intake by too much and simply was not eating enough for a period of time," she says. "I obviously began to eat more once I noticed the very tangible health repercussions caused by this, but this was a lesson I learned the hard way. A healthy diet (not too much and not too little!) and regular exercise is truly the best route to obtain and maintain your ideal weight."[71]

By making healthy food choices and getting regular physical activity, Morrison lost 40 pounds (18kg) over several months. Today she has turned her newfound love of cooking and creating healthy recipes into an award-winning healthy living website (www.foodiefiasco.com). Says Morrison:

> I am very careful about what I eat, but not because it's a chore—I love it! I also exercise nearly every day, and try to live the most active lifestyle I can within reason. I am on a much better level with myself in regards to my body image than I was to begin with, but I still have a long way to go. Some days are better than others, but I do love and respect myself exactly the way I am.[72]

Healthy Weight for a Lifetime

Finding a healthy weight can put teens on the path to better health. Taking small steps is a start in the right direction. Changing one snack, meal, or activity at a time can eventually lead to a more healthy weight. As registered dietitian Haley Lacey puts it, "Weight loss in the real world takes hard work, and focus should be on overall health, not on reaching a number on a scale."[73]

Introduction: Teens and Weight Loss

1. Haley Lacey. E-mail to the author, November 20, 2012.

Chapter 1: Healthy Weight and Body Image

2. Quoted in Kirsten Weir. "The Truth About Weight: Obesity Is a Big Challenge—but It Can Be Overcome." *Current Health Teens*, October 2011, p. 16.
3. Quoted in Weir. "The Truth About Weight," p. 16.
4. Kristi King. E-mail to the author, November 17, 2012.
5. King. E-mail.
6. Quoted in Jean Fain. "Lose Weight, Gain Body Confidence? Not Necessarily, Says Purdue Researcher Sarah Mustillo." *The Blog, Huffington Post*, May 24, 2012. www.huffingtonpost.com/jean-fain-licsw-msw/body-image_b_1541946.html.
7. Quoted in Temple University. "Ideal Weight Varies Across Cultures, but Body Image Dissatisfaction Pervades." ScienceDaily, October 24, 2007. www.sciencedaily.com/releases/2007/10/071023164042.htm.

8. Rebecca Clegg. E-mail to the author, November 19, 2012.
9. Lacey. E-mail.
10. Quoted in Reuters. "American Teen Girls Feel Pressure to Be Thin," February 1, 2010. www.reuters.com/article/2010/02/01/us-fashion-image-survey-idUSTRE6104Q420100201.
11. Quoted in Anne M. Fletcher. *Weight Loss Confidential*. Boston: Houghton Mifflin, 2006, p. 39.
12. Quoted in Fletcher. *Weight Loss Confidential*, p. 41.
13. Quoted in Val Wadas-Willingham. "New Program Helps Teen Girls with Weight Issues." *The Chart* (blog), CNN, February 13, 2012. http://thechart.blogs.cnn.com/2012/02/13/new-program-helps-teen-girls-with-weight-issues/?iref=allsearch.
14. Lacey. E-mail.

Chapter 2: Healthy Habits for a Healthy Weight

15. Quoted in Kathleen M. Zelman. "Teen Weight Loss Secrets." WebMD. www.webmd.com/diet/features/teen-weight-loss-secrets.
16. Dianne Neumark-Sztainer. *"I'm, Like, So Fat!" Helping Your Teen Make Healthy Choices About Eating*

and Exercise in a Weight-Obsessed World. New York: Guilford, 2005, p. 160.

17. Quoted in William Neuman. "Nutrition Plate Unveiled, Replacing Food Pyramid." New York Times, June 2, 2011. www.nytimes.com /2011/06/03/business/03plate .html?_r=0.

18. Quoted in Meredith Melnick. "The USDA Ditches the Food Pyramid for a Plate." Time, June 2, 2011. http://healthland.time .com/2011/06/02/the-usda-ditch es-the-food-pyramid-and-offers -a-plate.

19. Neumark-Sztainer. "I'm, Like, So Fat!" Helping Your Teen Make Healthy Choices About Eating and Exercise in a Weight-Obsessed World, p. 160.

20. Neumark-Sztainer. "I'm, Like, So Fat!" Helping Your Teen Make Healthy Choices About Eating and Exercise in a Weight-Obsessed World, p. 161.

21. Quoted in National Heart, Lung, and Blood Institute. "Larger Portion Sizes Contribute to U.S. Obesity Problem," May 8, 2012. www.nhlbi.nih.gov/health/public /heart/obesity/wecan/news-events /matte1.htm.

Chapter 3: Weight Loss Controversies—Fad Diets, Pills, and Surgery

22. King. E-mail.
23. King. E-mail.
24. Quoted in Taylor Orr. "Fad Diets: A Losing Battle." Pacific Standard, October 12, 2010. www.psmag.com /health/fad-diets-a-losing-battle -23918.

25. Quoted in Jane Shin Park. "Health Alert: The Dangers of Diet Pills." Teen Vogue, October 12, 2009. www .teenvogue.com/blog/teen-vogue -daily/2009/10/the-dangers-of-diet -pills.html.

26. Quoted in Orr. "Fad Diets."
27. Quoted in Rachel Garcia. "Fad Diet Disasters." Guardian, University of California–San Diego. www.ucsd guardian.org/calendar/item/4117 -faddietdisasters.

28. Lacey. E-mail.
29. Quoted in Madeline Vann. "The Facts on Fad Diets." EverydayHealth. com, November 16, 2012. www .everydayhealth.com/diet-nutrition /the-facts-on-fad-diets.aspx.

30. Clegg. E-mail.
31. Quoted in Park. "Health Alert."
32. Quoted in Park. "Health Alert."
33. Quoted in WINK News. "WINK Investigation Looks into Safety of Teen Diet Pills," May 16, 2012. www.winknews.com/Local-Flor ida/2012-05-15/WINK-investiga tion-looks-into-safety-of-teen-diet -pills.

34. Quoted in WINK News. "WINK Investigation Looks into Safety of Teen Diet Pills."

35. Quoted in Dan Childs. "Obesity Surgery for Weight Loss: A New Teenage Trend?" ABCNews.com, September

20, 2010. http://abcnews.go.com /Health/w_DietAndFitness/laparo scopic-banding-gastric-procedure -teens-rise/story?id=11671719#.UL -7Yndkia8.

36. Quoted in Eric Adler. "Weight Loss for Teens Becomes More Common." *Kansas City (MO) Star*, May 26, 2012.

37. Quoted in Anemona Hartocollis. "Young, Obese, and in Surgery." *New York Times*, January 7, 2012. www.nytimes.com/2012/01/08 /health/young-obese-and-getting -weight-loss-surgery.html?_r=0& adxnnl=1&pagewanted=all&adxn nlx=1354302311-Tx/uBQCMHB Ny00DQsulVTQ.

38. Quoted in ScienceDaily. "Gastric Bypass Surgery Just as Effective in Teenagers as in Adults, Study Suggests," October 22, 2012. www.sciencedaily.com/releases /2012/10/121022092934.htm.

39. Quoted in Anne Harding. "Surgery Is No Quick Fix for Obese Teens." CNN, June 22, 2011. www.cnn.com /2011/HEALTH/06/22/surgery .obese.teens/index.html.

40. Quoted in Harding. "Surgery Is No Quick Fix for Obese Teens."

41. Quoted in Randy Dotinga. "Gastric Band Surgery Rising Among Obese Teens." HealthDay, September 20, 2010. http://health.us news.com/health-news/managing -your-healthcare/treatment/articles /2010/09/20/gastric-band-surgery -rising-among-obese-teens.

Chapter 4: Weight Loss Gone Wrong

42. Quoted in Alan Mask. "Weight Loss Struggle Can Lead to Eating Disorders for Women." WRAL.com, January 8, 2007. www.wral.com/life styles/healthteam/story/1129984.

43. Jessica Setnick. E-mail to the author, November 19, 2012.

44. Neumark-Sztainer. *"I'm, Like, So Fat!" Helping Your Teen Make Healthy Choices About Eating and Exercise in a Weight-Obsessed World*, p. 104.

45. Setnick. E-mail.

46. Quoted in PRWeb. "One in 10 U.S. Teens Use Unhealthy Behaviors to Lose Weight," May 24, 2011. www .prweb.com/releases/eatingrecov erycenter/eatingdisordersinteen ager/prweb8473979.htm.

47. Lacey. E-mail.

48. Quoted in Fletcher. *Weight Loss Confidential*, p. 47.

49. Quoted in Randi Hutter Epstein. "Expert Q & A: Exploring Treatments for Eating Disorders." *New York Times*, July 13, 2009. www .nytimes.com/ref/health/health guide/esn-eating-disorders-expert .html?pagewanted=all.

50. National Eating Disorders Association. "Factors That May Contribute to Eating Disorders." www.nation aleatingdisorders.org/uploads/file /information-resources/Factors% 20that%20may%20Contribute%20 to%20Eating%20Disorders.pdf.

51. Quoted in Kim Carollo. "French Model Isabelle Caro's Death Highlights Tough Personal Battles Against Anorexia." ABCNews.com,

December 30, 2010. http://abcnews
.go.com/Health/MindMoodNews
/anti-anorexic-model-isabelle-caro
-dies/story?id=12509780&single
Page=true.

52. Quoted in Carollo. "French Model Isabelle Caro's Death Highlights Tough Personal Battles Against Anorexia."

53. Quoted in *Teen Vogue*. "Feeding Frenzy," February 2012, p. 114.

54. Quoted in *Teen Vogue*. "Feeding Frenzy," p. 114.

55. Quoted in Madison Park. "Inside One Boy's Anorexia: How Can I Burn the Most Calories?" CNN, December 3, 2010. www.cnn.com /2010/HEALTH/12/03/young.boys .anorexia/index.html.

56. Quoted in Park. "Inside One Boy's Anorexia."

Chapter 5: Living at a Healthy Weight

57. Quoted in Fletcher. *Weight Loss Confidential*, p. 86.

58. Centers for Disease Control and Prevention. "Healthy Eating for a Healthy Weight." www.cdc.gov /healthyweight/healthy_eating /index.html.

59. Lacey. E-mail.

60. Quoted in Fletcher. *Weight Loss Confidential*, p. 139.

61. Quoted in Madeline Vann. "Why Skipping Meals Undermines Weight Loss." EverydayHealth.com, June 8, 2010. www.everydayhealth.com /weight/skipping-meals-under mines-weight-loss.aspx.

62. Quoted in Vann. "Why Skipping Meals Undermines Weight Loss."

63. Quoted in Laura Stroop and Deane Morrison. "Champions of Break- fast." University of Minnesota, March 4, 2008. www1.umn.edu /news/features/2008f/UR_174872 _REGION1.html.

64. King. E-mail.

65. Quoted in Fletcher. *Weight Loss Confidential*, p. 150.

66. Quoted in University of Illinois College of Agricultural, Consum- er and Environmental Sciences. "Family Meals Remain Impor- tant Through Teen Years, Expert Says." ScienceDaily, July 13, 2011. www.sciencedaily.com/releases /2011/07/110712162828.htm.

67. King. E-mail.

68. Quoted in Alice Oglethorpe. "'This Time Was Different.' Michelle Lost 46 Pounds." *Shape*. www.shape.com /weight-loss/success-stories/time -was-different-michelle-lost-46 -pounds.

69. Quoted in Fletcher. *Weight Loss Confidential*, p. 167.

70. Setnick. E-mail.

71. Kelly Morrison. E-mail to the author, November 23, 2012.

72. Morrison. E-mail.

73. Lacey. E-mail.

bariatric: Of or relating to the treatment of obesity, such as in bariatric surgery.

body image: An individual's concept of his or her own body.

body mass index (BMI): A calculation that uses a person's height and weight to estimate how much body fat he or she has.

calorie: A unit used to measure the energy value of food. One calorie is the amount of heat (energy) required to warm 1 gram of water 1 degree Celsius.

chronic: Occurring for a long time.

dietitian: A person who is an expert in nutrition and diets.

epidemic: A rapid spread or the increase in occurrence of something, like a disease.

fad diet: A diet plan that promises dramatic weight loss in a short time.

gastric: Related to the stomach.

monounsaturated fatty acid: an unsaturated fatty acid that comes from plants and vegetables. This type of fat is considered healthy and can lower bad cholesterol levels.

nutrients: Components of food, like vitamins and minerals, that are necessary for growth and life.

obese: Extremely fat or overweight. An adult with a BMI of 30 or higher is considered obese.

polyunsaturated fatty acid: an unsaturated fat that comes from plants and vegetables. This type of fat is found in safflower, sesame, and corn oils.

portion: An amount of food served for one person in one sitting.

saturated fat: a fat that is solid at room temperature, usually from animal products such as meat, eggs, and dairy. Saturated fat directly raises cholesterol levels.

trans fat: a type of fat that is typically used to extend the shelf life of processed foods such as cookies and cakes. Trans fat can raise cholesterol levels.

Academy of Nutrition and Dietetics

120 S. Riverside Plaza, Ste. 2000
Chicago, IL 60606-6995
(800) 877-1600
www.eatright.org

The Academy of Nutrition and Dietetics is the world's largest organization of food and nutrition professionals. The academy's website features timely, science-based food and nutrition information.

Campaign for a Commercial-Free Childhood (CCFC)

NonProfit Center
89 South St., Ste. 403
Boston, MA 02111
(617) 896-9368
fax: (617) 896-9377
http://commercialfreechildhood.org

The CCFC is a national coalition of health-care professionals, educators, advocacy groups, parents, and individuals devoted to limiting the impact of the commercial culture on children. The CCFC website provides information about the debate over the effect of media on body image and eating disorders.

Center for Science in the Public Interest

1220 L St. NW, Ste. 300
Washington, DC 20005
(202) 332-9110
fax: (202) 265-4954
www.cspinet.org

The Center for Science in the Public Interest is an advocate for nutrition and health, food safety, alcohol policy, and sound science. It circulates a newsletter, and its website offers many resources for the latest news and science related to nutrition.

National Eating Disorders Association

165 W. Forty-Sixth St., Ste. 402
New York, NY 10036
(212) 575-6200
www.nationaleatingdisorders.org

The National Eating Disorders Association is a nonprofit organization dedicated to supporting individuals and families affected by eating disorders. The association's website offers a variety of information about eating disorders, research, and programs.

U.S. Department of Agriculture Center for Nutrition Policy and Promotion

3101 Park Center Dr., 10th Fl.
Alexandria, VA 22302-1594
(703) 305-7600
fax: (703) 305-3300
www.cnpp.usda.gov

The Center for Nutrition Policy and Promotion is part of the Department of Agriculture. Its goal is to improve the nutrition and well-being of Americans. The center's staff of nutritionists and dietitians can answer basic food and nutrition questions.

Books

Leslie J. Favor. *Food as Foe: Nutrition and Eating Disorders.* Tarrytown, NY: Marshall Cavendish, 2010. This book provides a short overview of nutrition and eating disorders.

Leslie J. Favor. *Weighing In: Nutrition and Weight Management.* Tarrytown, NY: Marshall Cavendish, 2010. This book provides a short overview about nutrition and weight management.

Anne M. Fletcher. *Weight Loss Confidential.* Boston: Houghton Mifflin, 2006. This book provides sensible nutrition advice from teens to teens and parents.

Jodie Shield and Mary Catherine Mullen. *Healthy Eating, Healthy Weight for Kids and Teens.* Chicago: Eat Right, 2012. This book written by registered dietitians shares strategies to help children and teens reach a healthier weight.

Internet Sources

Courtney Hutchenson. "Weight Loss Surgery Best Option for Overweight Teens?" ABCNews.com, February 10, 2010. http://abcnews.go.com/Health /Wellness/teen-weight-loss-surgery -gastric-bands-worth-risk/story ?id=9786842.

William Neuman. "Nutrition Plate Unveiled, Replacing Food Pyramid." *New York Times*, June 2, 2011. www .nytimes.com/2011/06/03/business /03plate.html?_r=1&.

Websites

Centers for Disease Control and Prevention (www.cdc.gov). This website is a central place to research nutrition, healthy eating, and the diseases and conditions that unhealthy eating can trigger, like obesity, heart disease, and diabetes.

ChooseMyPlate.gov, U.S. Department of Agriculture (www.choosemyplate. gov). This website offers interactive tools, menu planners, podcasts, and information about healthy eating.

Food-a-pedia (www.supertracker .usda.gov/foodapedia.aspx). Part of the Department of Agriculture's SuperTracker website, this page provides quick access to food information. Find calories and food groups for a food, or compare two foods.

Healthy Eating, Food Network (www .foodnetwork.com/healthy-eating /index.html). The healthy eating section of the Food Network website features recipes for low-fat cooking, whole grains, favorite recipe makeovers, and vegetarian and healthy snacks.

How to Understand and Use the Nutrition Facts Label, U.S. Food and Drug Administration (www.fda.gov/food /ResourcesForYou/Consumers/NFL PM/ucm274593.htm). This site presents information about understanding and using the nutrition facts label on food products.

KidsHealth (www.kidshealth.org). This website offers kids' and teens' sections that have information about healthy eating and nutrition. Learn about food labels, fats, proteins, and carbohydrates. The site also offers healthy recipes to try.

Nutrition.com (www.nutrition.com). Nutrition.com offers pages for children and teens with information about healthy eating. There is nutrition information on several fast food restaurants. Teens can also try the nutrition calculators to figure out their BMI, waist-to-hip ratio, and estimated daily calorie needs.

INDEX

A

Adolescents. *See* Children/
adolescents

Adults
benefits of weight loss surgery
for, 52
interpretation of BMI in, 16
percentage underweight, 12
prevalence of obesity among, 11
use of weight loss drugs by,
48–50

American Academy of Pediatrics,
51

Anorexia nervosa, 60, 62, 64–66

Appetite suppressants, 48–49

Atkins, Robert, 43

Atkins diet, 43

B

Bariatric surgery, 51–52, 53
for adolescents, 53–55
eating habits following, 55–56
health risks of, 52–53

Binge eating disorder, 60

BMI. *See* Body mass index

Body image, 17–18
impact of media on, 19–21

Body mass index (BMI), 15–17
in determining candidates for
weight loss, 24, 48

Boys, eating disorders among,
70–72

Breakfast, percentage of teens
skipping, 84

Bulimia nervosa, 60, 66–68

C

Calcium, 76

Calorie(s), 27
in Big Mac sandwich, 29
effects of severely restricting,
44
empty, 81
leading source of, 36

Carbohydrates, complex, 76

Cardiovascular disease,
percentage of obese youth and,
17

Catecholamine, 48–49

Centers for Disease Control and
Prevention (CDC), 11, 12,
57–58, 76
pediatric growth charts of, 12
on size of average woman, 19

G

Girl Scout Research Institute, 19
Girls/women
    eating disorders among, 64,
      69–70
    media pressures on, 19–21
Grains, 30
    recommended serving sizes of,
      33, 37
Growth/development, effects of
    food restriction on, 46

H

Health risks
    of anorexia, 65–66
    of bariatric surgery, 52–53
    of bulimia, 67–68
    of fad diets, 44–47
    of obesity, 12–13
    of weight loss drugs, 49–50
    of weight loss supplements,
      48
Health weight, factors in, 14
Healthy eating
    definition of, 28–29
    as most effective for
      maintaining healthy weight,
      47
    tips for, 73–76

I

International Journal of Obesity,
    54–55

J

*Journal of Nutrition Education and
    Behavior,* 82

L

Lacey, Helen, 60, 76–77
    on fad diets, 46
    on importance of gradual
      weight loss, 24–25
    on media, 19
    on teens' need to focus on
      health, 10, 88
Lap-Band, 53

M

Malnutrition, from weight loss
    surgery, 54
Media, body images promoted by,
    8, 19–21
Metabolism, effects of restricted-
    calorie diets on, 45
MyPlate, *30*, 31–32
    recommended serving sizes
      under, 33

N

National Alliance on Mental
    Illness, 64, 66
National Center for Health
    Statistics, 12
National Eating Disorders
    Association, 58, 69

National Institutes of Health, 35
National Youth Risk Behavior
  Survey (Centers for Disease
  Control and Prevention),
  57–58
Nutrients
  fad diets and, 39
  health risks of lack of, 44
  importance of breakfast in
    getting, 79
  lack of, in empty-calorie foods,
    81
  weight loss surgery and, 52,
    54
Nutrition labels, 23, *23*

O

Obama, Michelle, 32
Obesity/overweight
  among teenagers, *12*
  health risks of, 12–13
  prevalence of, 11
Oils. *See* Fats/oils
Ornish diet, 43

P

Pediatric growth charts, 14
Pediatrics (journal), 82
Physical activity, 83–85
  regular, importance of,
    38–39
Physical Activity Guidelines for
  Americans (Department of

Health and Human Services),
  39
Portion sizes, 8
  of fast food, increase in, 36
  increases in, 35
  serving sizes *vs.*, 36–37
  visual guidelines for, *35*
Potassium deficiency, 67–68
Proteins, 30–31
  recommended serving sizes of,
    33

R

Race/ethnicity, as factor in body
  image, 17–18

S

Salt, 76
Sedentary lifestyle, 8–9
Serotonin, 48–49
Serving sizes, 33, 34
  factors in, 34, 36
  portion sizes *vs.*, 36–37
  visual guidelines for, 38
Supplements, weight loss, 47–48,
  49
Surgery, weight loss. *See* Bariatric
  surgery
Surveys, of teenage girls, 20–21

U

Underweight, prevalence of, 12

PICTURE CREDITS

ABOUT THE AUTHOR

Carla Mooney received her undergraduate degree in economics from the University of Pennsylvania. She has written many books for young people, including *Junk Food Junkies*, which are part of Lucent Books' Nutrition and Health series. Mooney lives with her husband and three children in Pittsburgh, Pennsylvania.